Encyclopedia of
Continental Army Units

Washington, D. C.

To Whom It May Concern:

The Company of Military Historians through its Review Board

takes pleasure in sponsoring ENCYCLOPEDIA OF CONTINENTAL ARMY UNITS--

battalions, regiments and independent corps as an accurate and useful

work in American military history.

James C. Hazlett, M. D.
President

Review Board

Detmar H. Finke

Harold L. Peterson

Marko Zlatich

Henry I. Shaw, Jr., Editor in Chief

Encyclopedia of
Continental Army Units

Battalions, Regiments and Independent Corps

by Fred Anderson Berg

STACKPOLE BOOKS

ENCYCLOPEDIA OF CONTINENTAL ARMY UNITS
—battalions, regiments and independent corps

Copyright©1972 by
THE STACKPOLE COMPANY
Published by
STACKPOLE BOOKS
Cameron and Kelker Streets
Harrisburg, Pennsylvania 17105

Printed in the U.S.A.

Library of Congress Cataloging in Publication Data

Berg, Fred Anderson, 1948-
    Encyclopedia of Continental Army units--battalions, regiments, and independent corps.

    Bibliography: p.
    1. U. S. Army. Continental Army--Directories.
I. Title.
E259.B47   973.3'4'025   70-38505
ISBN 0-8117-0544-7

CONTENTS

86275

How to Use This Book

This book gives a compact organizational history of each battalion, regiment and independent corps that served in the Continental Army. The book also includes some information on the larger organizational elements of the Continental Army as well as information on certain militia and state troops helpful to historians and those using it as a reference.

During the period of the American Revolution people were not so precise as we today in spelling or in employing organizational nomenclature. Thus Bedel, Beedel, Beetle, and Beedell are all spellings of the same person's name just as the 3rd Regiment of Continental Light Dragoons, Baylor's Dragoons, and the Corps of Baylor all refer to the same unit. The practice of those days was still to call a unit after its commander's name rather than by a number or letter so for that reason—even when a unit was numbered—I have mentioned the name of its commander and the dates within which he was associated with the unit.

The dates of the commander's service were taken largely from Francis B. Heitman's *Historical Register of Officers of the Continental Army*. It should be noted some of the commissions were predated or postdated. During the Revolution the terms regiment and battalion were often used interchangeably. I have chosen to use the term regiment for all infantry units of such size unless there is no evidence that they were so called. Unless otherwise mentioned, the reader may assume that the unit discussed was ordinary line infantry, the word infantry seldom appearing in the designation of a Revolutionary War foot soldier unit. No battle honors are listed for the various units in this book as information is often unclear covering just what organizations were engaged in each battle, and battle honors are anyway often misleading.

This book is organized in encyclopedic fashion, the units being described in alphabetical order. Alphabetizing has not been easy and the author begs the readers' understanding in the matter. As a convenience to the reader an alphabetical index of commanders' names is included at the end of the book. The reader should note that many commanders were related and therefore the full name of any officer being "looked up" should be noted.

A

Albemarle County Battalion   Authorized January 9, 1779 by Congress to serve one year. The battalion was to guard the prisoners from Saratoga that were held in Virginia. It was to be liable for service only in Albemarle County. The battalion was to have a staff of 1 ensign, 1 surgeon, and 1 surgeon's mate, and eight companies. Each company was to have 1 company commander (one of whom was a lieutenant colonel commandant, one a major, and the other six captains), 1 lieutenant (called a captain lieutenant in the lieutenant colonel's company), 1 ensign, 3 sergeants, 1 drummer, 1 fifer, and 70 corporals and privates.[1] This unit may actually have been one and the same as Colonel Francis Taylor's Virginia State Regiment of Convention Guards of 1779-1781. Note the term convention referred to the surrender convention of Saratoga. (See also State Troops, Virginia; Virginia State Troops Guarding the Convention Prisoners.)

Armand's Legion   On June 11, 1777 Lieutenant Colonel Charles Armand Tuffin, Marquis de la Rouerie, succeeded to the command of Baron Ottendorf's Independent Company (which see).[2] Armand was an officer in the French Army. By November of that year the unit had picked up a quartermaster and a surgeon, but was down to 42 privates. Armand knew if word got around that his unit was so small it would probably be broken up so he initiated a recruiting drive. His recruiters brought in their share of wretched characters, including German prisoners of war. On June 25, 1778 Congress officially authorized Armand's recruiting methods.[3] Armand's "Free and Independent Chasseurs" was to have 1 colonel, 1 major, 1 ensign major (a standard bearer paid as a lieutenant), and three companies each of 1 captain, 1 captain lieutenant, 2 lieutenants, 8 sergeants, 8 corporals, 2 drummers, and 128 privates. Foreign officers were allowed as were German deserters in the ranks. As actually organized in August, 1778, Armand's Partisan Corps had 1 colonel, 1 lieutenant colonel, 4 captains, 3 lieutenants, 1 adjutant, 1 quartermaster, 1 surgeon, 1 surgeon's mate, 1 sergeant major, 1 quartermaster sergeant, 1 drum major, 12 sergeants, 4 fifers and drummers, and 121 privates.

In late 1778 a troop of dragoons was added to the corps so that in January, 1779 Armand's Legion had one troop of dragoons of 3 officers and 42 troopers, two companies of fusiliers each of 2 officers and 46 men, and one company of chasseurs (riflemen?) of 3 officers and 80 men. The legion was largely German deserters and on June 21, 1779 a Corps of German Volunteers was incorporated into the unit.[4] In 1780 the legion is listed as 60 horse and 60 footmen. The legion was ordered reorganized on November 1, 1780 as three horse and three foot troops by January 1, 1781. Congress further authorized Armand to take up to six men from each Continental regiment to fill his corps.

Armand's Legion served in many battles in the South in 1780-81, yet observers constantly remarked on its ill discipline. Major Henry Lee said that the French officers of the unit were gallant enough, but he spoke with loathing of the German deserters and other scoundrels they led.[5] In 1782 Armand's Legion is said to have been 200 strong and over 300 strong the next year. The corps served until October 29, 1783[6] and was actually not disbanded until November 25 of that year.[7] As one of the largest units remaining in the army in 1783 and one of the last to be disbanded, it is little wonder that Congress so feared an armed coup d'état. It is peculiar that such a corps was ever raised, let alone supported by public funds for so long.

COMMANDER: Lieutenant Colonel Charles Armand Tuffin, Marquis de la Rouerie June 11, 1777-November 25, 1783. Armand was made a brigadier general on March 26, 1783.

American Legion   *See* Count Beniousky's American Legion.

1st American Regiment   *See* Jackson's Continental Regiment.

Arnold's Canadian Expeditionary Force   To cooperate with the forces of the Separate Army (which see) invading Canada, General Washington detached around 1300 men under Colonel Benedict Arnold. This force was formed about September 1, 1775 and consisted of thirteen companies of volunteers from the New England regiments around Boston and several Virginia and Pennsylvania rifle companies. The expedition did link up with the Separate Army and participated in the assault on Quebec. After the failure of this attack, the survivors were largely absorbed into the Northern Army (which see.)[8]

Artificers   *See* Regiment of Artillery Artificers; Staff Departments, Quartermaster Department.

Artillery   *See* Corps of Continental Artillery.

Regiment of Artillery Artificers   On January 16, 1777 Washington requested Colonel Flower, the Commissary General of Military Stores, to raise several units of artificers (workmen) which came to be called Flower's Regiment. Washington wanted an artillery shop in Pennsylvania of 49 carpenters, 40 blacksmiths, 20 wheelwrights, tinners, and turners, and 12 harnessmakers. The general also wanted a laboratory company of 1 captain, 1 captain lieutenant, 4 lieutenants, 6 sergeants, 6 corporals, 1 drummer, 1 fifer, 6 bombardiers, and 28 mattrosses. Finally, Washington wished a company of artificers to serve in the field with the Corps of Artillery. This company consisted of a master carpenter (company commander), master wheelwright, master blacksmith, 2 tin men, 2 turners, 2 coopers, 4 harnessmakers, 2 nailers, 2 farriers, 6 wheelwrights, 25 carpenters, and 15 smiths. The men in the artillery shop were to be enlisted for one year, the remainder for the war.[9] In February, Flower enlisted a field company under Captain Rowe, two depot companies under Captains Irish and Pancoast, and a laboratory under Captain

Curren, all of which were to serve for the war.[10] Thus Flower did not follow Washington's request to the letter. January 8, 1778, Washington requested the laboratories at Springfield and Carlisle be increased to 100 men each.[11] On February 11, 1778 Captain Wylie was instructed to raise an additional company.[12]

Since November 16, 1776, long before Flower's Regiment was created, there had been a company of artillery artificers in the Northern Army under Captain Noah Nichols. In November, 1778 Nichols' company merged with Rowe's company, Nichols assuming command.[13]

It is difficult to understand just what jobs the Artillery Artificers performed. Probably their role was that of the modern Ordnance Department—the supervision of manufacture, conversion, maintenance, and repair of weapons and vehicles. Then, as now, some of these duties overlapped those of the Quartermaster Department so it is likely that the regiment of artificers placed on the Pennsylvania quota in November, 1780 was intended to include both artillery and quartermaster artificers *(see* Staff Departments). The tiny artillery artificers companies did not go through this merger smoothly and the net result was a loss for both the Corps of Artillery and the Quartermaster Department. It seems that a few individual artillery artificers, however, remained with the Corps of Artillery until the end of the war.

COMMANDER: Colonel Benjamin Flower January 16, 1777-April 28, 1781.

B

Baldwin's Regiment of Quartermaster Artificers   *See* Staff Departments, Quartermaster Department.

Bateaux Service   *See* Staff Departments, Quartermaster Department.

Captain Bauman's Independent Artillery Company   Raised in New York after March 30, 1776. When it entered the Continental service is not clear, but on January 1, 1777 Bauman was commissioned to reorganize his company as a part of the 2nd Battalion of Continental Artillery (which see).

> COMMANDER: Captain Sebastian Bauman State commission dated March 30, 1776. Continental commission dated January 1, 1777.

Bedford County Volunteers   Three ranger companies were raised to defend the Pennsylvania frontier. They were probably first raised sometime before mid-1778. On November 5, 1778 they were to be reenlisted till December 15, 1779 and payed by Congress.[14]

COMPANY COMMANDERS NOVEMBER 5, 1778:
Captain Thomas Cluggage
Captain Henry Black
Captain John McDonald

COMPANY COMMANDERS APRIL 7, 1779[15]:
Captain Thomas Cluggage
Captain Camble
Captain Erwin

Evidently the corps had to be completely reorganized in 1779.

Count Beniousky's American Legion   On May 24, 1782 Congress accepted the proffered services of Count Beniousky's Legion. Beniousky's force was then reputedly gathered in France in three corps totalling 3,483 men. They were to sail for America as soon as possible. The Legion was, of course, a collection of mercenaries of all nationalities. Congress seemed eager to receive these reenforcements, commenting that after hostilities ceased the soldiers would become useful new citizens of the United States. It is possible they would have, many former British and German soldiers did, but as a mass of armed foreigners on American soil and in numbers amounting to a third of the dwindling Continental Army it is in fact, perhaps best these men never sailed.[16] On May 29, 1782 Congress refused Beniousky's services only five days after it had initially accepted them.

Captain Bigelow's Independent Artillery Company   Bigelow's company was a Connecticut unit raised for Continental service in the Northern Department in early 1776. It served there through the year, some of its men later serving in Stevens' Battalion (which see).[17]

COMMANDER: Captain John Bigelow January 19, 1776-December, 1776.

Bradley's Battalion of Connecticut State Troops   Served at Trenton in December, 1776. This was not a Continental unit.

COMMANDER: Colonel Philip Burr Bradley May-December 1776.

Captain William Brown's Maryland Artillery Company   In October, 1777 Congress asked to borrow Maryland's artillery companies.[18] These companies of mattrosses had been raised early in 1776 by the state. On November 22, 1777 Congress accordingly voted to take Brown's and Dorsey's companies into its pay[19] and by March, 1778 these companies had set out to join the Main Army where they were already assigned to the 1st Battalion of Continental Artillery.[20] On September 3, 1779 this company merged with Dorsey's.[21]

COMMANDER: Captain William Brown Continental commission dated November 20, 1777.

Captain Bartholomew Burke's United States Company   Authorized March 4, 1777 with a strength of 4 sergeants, 1 drummer, 1 fifer, and 68 rank and file. No further information.[22]

Colonel Burrall's Connecticut Regiment   January 8, 1776 Congress resolved that Connecticut should furnish a battalion for the defense of Canada.[23] Accordingly, Burrall's Regiment was enlisted for one year until January 19, 1777. The regiment served in Canada, two of its companies being captured at the Cedars on May 19, 1776. The remnants of the regiment were discharged in early 1777. Some early sources call this a state regiment, but this is incorrect.[24]

COMMANDER: Colonel Charles Burrall January 19, 1776-January 19, 1777.

C

1st Canadian Regiment   On November 10, 1775 Congress issued instructions for General Schuyler to raise a Canadian battalion in the Continental pay.[25] By December 23 of that year a regiment of Canadians had indeed been raised by Colonel James Livingston.[26] After long service, Livingston's regiment was broken up by General Orders effective January 1, 1781. Many of Livingston's former soldiers went into Hazen's Regiment (see 2nd Canadian Regiment).

COMMANDER: Colonel James Livingston November 20, 1775-January 1, 1781.

2nd Canadian Regiment   January 20, 1776 Congress voted ro raise 1,000 additional Canadians. These were to be formed into a regiment consisting of 1 colonel, 1 lieutenant colonel, and four battalions. Each battalion was to have a major and five companies each of 1 captain, 1 lieutenant, 1 ensign, and 50 men.[27] Actually it is doubtful that the regiment formed over one battalion. On January 22, Moses Hazen was elected to command the regiment.

Hazen's Canadian Regiment was engaged in the retreat across New Jersey in the fall of 1776. Already it seems to have had a light company and to have acquired the title of "Congress's Own Regiment". In subsequent years the regiment was often referred to as Congress's Own as Congress, itself, had to see that the regiment was supplied and maintained. In 1777 the regiment was reorganized to include two companies from Maryland[28] and a company from Connecticut.[29] Most of its personnel, however, remained foreigners.

In General Orders effective January 1, 1781 all foreigners in the Continental service (presumably Armand's Corps excepted) were to be taken into Hazen's Regiment. It was hoped that this would make it a two battalion unit, but this hope seems to have been too high.[30] The regiment continued to maintain a good reputation despite its numerous foreigners. December 25, 1782 Washington proposed to recruit German prisoners of war into the regiment,[31] but nothing came of this, nor of his earlier June, 1782 proposal to disband the regiment and form the French Canadians in it into a company of watermen.[32] June 9, 1783 Hazen's Regiment was disbanded by Congress.[33] Hazen's Regiment seems to have had an exceptionally good record, yet like the miserable Legion of Armand, the regiment was largely foreigners.

COMMANDER: Colonel Moses Hazen January 22, 1776-June, 1783. During 1781 the regiment was usually actually commanded by Lieutenant Colonel Edward Antil.

Captain Carberry's Troop of Light Horse   This troop was reputedly raised out of the 11th Pennsylvania Regiment about December, 1778. No further information. Carberry was mortally wounded in January, 1779.

Captain Catherwood's Independent Company   Raised in Pennsylvania. Incorporated into the 11th Pennsylvania Regiment on January 13, 1779[34] having formerly been attached to Malcolm's Additional Continental Regiment.[35]

Congress's Own Regiment   *See* 2nd Canadian Regiment.

Connecticut Garrison Companies   June 24, 1776 Congress authorized Connecticut to raise three garrison companies at Continental expense in the New London area.[36]

Connecticut Light Horse   *See* 2nd Regiment of Continental Light Dragoons; Hyde's Connecticut Light Horse; Seymour's Connecticut Light Horse.

1st Connecticut Regiment of 1775

1st Connecticut Regiment of 1775   The 1st Connecticut was one of six regiments created by the Connecticut legislature on May 1, 1775. Each regiment was to have ten companies each of 1 captain or field grade officer, 2 lieutenants, 1 ensign, 4 sergeants, 4 corporals, 1 drummer, 1 fifer, and 100 privates.[37] By resolve of Congress on June 14, 1775 the six Connecticut regiments were taken into the Continental Army. The regiments served until mid-December of 1775 when most of the Connecticut men went home on the expiration of their enlistments.

COMMANDERS: Colonel David Wooster May 1, 1775-June 25, 1775. Lieutenant Colonel Andrew Ward June 25, 1775-December 20, 1775.

1st Connecticut Regiment of 1777   This regiment was organized in the early part of 1777 and served until the massive reorganization of the Connecticut Line on January 1, 1781 when most of its personel went into the new 5th Connecticut Regiment.[38]

COMMANDERS: Colonel Jedediah Huntington January 1, 1777-May 12, 1777.
Lieutenant Colonel Samuel Prentice May 12, 1777-May 27, 1778.
Colonel Josiah Starr May 27, 1778-January 1, 1781.

1st Connecticut Regiment of 1781   Formed January 1, 1781 from the old 3rd and 4th Connecticut Regiments and served until about June 3, 1783 when its veterans were furloughed and its recruits formed into the sole remaining Connecticut Regiment.[39]

COMMANDERS: Colonel John Durkee January 1, 1781-May 29, 1782.
Lieutenant Colonel Thomas Grosvenor May 29, 1782-January 1, 1783.
Colonel Zebulon Butler January 1, 1783-June, 1783.

2nd Connecticut Regiment of 1775   The organizational history of this regiment was identical to that of the 1st Connecticut Regiment of 1775 (which see).

COMMANDERS: Colonel Joseph Spencer May 1, 1775-June 25, 1775.
Lieutenant Colonel Samuel Wyllys June 25, 1775-December 10, 1775. Wyllys promoted to colonel July 1, 1775.

2nd Connecticut Regiment of 1777   Organized in early 1777 and served until the reorganization of January 1, 1781 at which time most of its personel went into the new 3rd Connecticut Regiment.

COMMANDERS: Colonel Charles Webb January 1, 1777-March 13, 1778.
Colonel Zebulon Butler March 13, 1778-January 1, 1781.

2nd Connecticut Regiment of 1781   The new 2nd Connecticut Regiment was formed January 1, 1781 from the remnants of the old 5th and 7th Connecticut Regiments. The regiment served until around June 3, 1783 when its veterans were furloughed and its recruits pooled with those of the other Connecticut regiments to form the sole remaining Connecticut Regiment.

COMMANDER: Colonel Heman Swift January 1, 1781-June 3, 1783.

3rd Connecticut Regiment of 1775   The organizational history of this regiment was identical with the 1st Connecticut Regiment of 1775 (which see).

COMMANDERS: Colonel Israel Putnam May 1, 1775-June 19, 1775.
Lieutenant Colonel Experience Storrs June 19, 1775-December 10, 1775. Storrs was promoted to colonel on July 1, 1775.

3rd Connecticut Regiment of 1777   Organized in early 1777 and served until the reorganization of January 1, 1781 when most of its personel were incorporated into the new 1st Connecticut Regiment.

COMMANDER: Colonel Samuel Wyllys January 1, 1777-January 1, 1781.

3rd Connecticut Regiment of 1781   Created on January 1, 1781 by a merger of the former 2nd and 9th Connecticut Regiments. The regiment served until around June 3, 1783 when its veterans were furloughed and its recruits pooled into the sole surviving Connecticut Regiment.

COMMANDER: Colonel Samuel B. Webb January 1, 1781-June, 1783.

4th Connecticut Regiment of 1775   The organizational history of this regiment was identical with the 1st Connecticut Regiment of 1775 (which see). Two companies from this regiment were garrisoned at Fort Ticondaroga.

COMMANDER: Colonel Benjamin Hyman (Hinman) May 1, 1775-December 20, 1775.

4th Connecticut Regiment of 1777   Organized in early 1777 and served until the reorganization of January 1, 1781 when most of its personnel were incorporated into the new 1st Connecticut Regiment.

COMMANDER: Colonel John Durkee January 1, 1777-January 1, 1781.

4th Connecticut Regiment of 1781   Formed January 1, 1781 by redesignating the old 6th Connecticut. Served until January 1, 1783 when it was broken up. Half its remaining enlisted men were incorporated into the 1st Connecticut Regiment; half into the 3rd Connecticut Regiment.

COMMANDER: Colonel Zebulon Butler January 1, 1781-January 1, 1783.

5th Connecticut Regiment of 1775   The organizational history of this regiment was identical with that of the 1st Connecticut Regiment of 1775 (which see).

COMMANDER: Colonel David Waterbury May 1, 1775-December 13, 1775.

5th Connecticut Regiment of 1777   Organized in early 1777 and served until the reorganization of January 1, 1781 when its remaining personel were incorporated into the new 2nd Connecticut Regiment.

COMMANDER: Colonel Philip Bradley January 1, 1777-January 1, 1781.

5th Connecticut Regiment of 1781   Formed January 1, 1781 from the men of the old 1st and 8th Connecticut Regiments and served until January 1, 1783 when its remaining enlisted men were incorporated into the 2nd Connecticut Regiment.

COMMANDER: Lieutenant Colonel Isaac Sherman January 1, 1781-January 1, 1783.

6th Connecticut Regiment of 1775   The organizational history of this regiment was identical with the 1st Connecticut Regiment of 1775 (which see).

COMMANDER: Colonel Samuel Parsons May 1, 1775-December 10, 1775.

6th Connecticut Regiment of 1777   Organized in early 1777 and served until the reorganization of January 1, 1781 when it was redesignated the 4th Connecticut Regiment.

COMMANDERS: Colonel William Douglas January 1, 1777-May 28, 1778.
Colonel Return Meigs May 12, 1777-January 1, 1781.

7th Connecticut Regiment of 1775   This regiment was created July 6, 1775 by the Connecticut legislature and served in the Continental Army until mid-December, 1775. It was organized like the 1st Connecticut Regiment of 1775 (which see), but was to have only 70 privates per company.[40]

COMMANDER: Colonel Charles Webb July 6, 1775-December 10, 1775.

7th Connecticut Regiment of 1777   Organized in early 1777 and served until the reorganization of January 1, 1781 when its remaining personnel were incorporated into the new 2nd Connecticut Regiment.

COMMANDER: Colonel Heman Swift January 1, 1777-January 1, 1781.

8th Connecticut Regiment of 1775   This regiment had an organizational history identical to the 7th Connecticut Regiment of 1775 (which see).

COMMANDER: Colonel Jedediah Huntington July 6, 1775-December 10, 1775.

8th Connecticut Regiment of 1777   Organized in early 1777 and served until the reorganization of January 1, 1781 when its remnants were incorporated into the new 5th Connecticut Regiment.

COMMANDERS: Colonel John Chandler January 1, 1777-March 5, 1778.

21

Colonel Giles Russell March 5, 1778-October 28, 1779.
Lieutenant Colonel Isaac Sherman October 28, 1779-January 1, 1781.

9th Connecticut Regiment   July 18, 1780, Samuel B. Webb's Additional Continental Regiment was taken into Connecticut's quota for the next campaign and accordingly numbered as the 9th Connecticut Regiment. Its service under that designation was short, however, as during the reorganization of the Connecticut Line on January 1, 1781 it was incorporated into the new 3rd Connecticut Regiment.

COMMANDER: Colonel Samuel B. Webb July 18, 1780-January 1, 1781.

Connecticut Regiment   After June 3, 1783 the newer enlistees in the Connecticut Line were formed into a regiment which served until November 25, 1783 when the remnants of the Continental Army marched into New York City and then were disbanded.

COMMANDER: Colonel Heman Swift June 3, 1783-December 25, 1783.

Continental Army   The army of the forces from four New England colonies encamped around Boston in June, 1775 was taken into the service of the "Continent" on June 14. This was the original Continental Army, the other forces in the pay and service of the Continental Congress were originally differently designated. Soon, however, all forces in the service and pay of Congress came to be considered alike as parts of the Continental Army.

Corps of Continental Artillery   This designation had two different definitions. It was applied at times to all the artillerists in the Continental service and at times limited to Knox's Brigade of Artillery with the Main Army 1777-1783 and Crane's (later Bauman's) corps with that body in 1783-1784.

Knox's brigade was formed of a small staff consisting of himself, 1 brigade major, 1 chaplain, and later on a quartermaster and an inspector; a company of the Regiment of Artillery Artificers (which see); attached civilian teamsters; four regiments or battalions of varying strength; and sometimes several more or less independent companies.

The four battalions (sometimes termed regiments) of artillery were each divided into several companies. Battalions, and to a lesser extent companies, were administrative and drill units only and they were never employed as tactical entities in the field. There was no standardized battalion organization set down until May 27, 1778 when an artillery battalion was ordered to consist of:

STAFF:	1 colonel, 1 lieutenant colonel, 1 major, 1 surgeon, 1 surgeon's mate, 1 sergeant major, 1 quartermaster sergeant, 1 drum major, 1 fife major
12 COMPANIES: EACH	1 captain, 1 captain lieutenant, 1 1st lieutenant, 3 2nd lieutenants, 6 sergeants, 6 corporals, 1 drummer, 1 fifer, 6 gunners, 6 bombardiers, 28 mattrosses
TOTAL:	729 officers and men

The adjutant, quartermaster, and paymaster of the battalion were lieutenants doing double duty.

The organization was changed in the General Order effective January 1, 1781 to:

STAFF:	1 colonel, 1 lieutenant colonel, 1 major, 1 adjutant, 1 quartermaster, 1 paymaster, 1 surgeon, 1 surgeon's mate, 1 sergeant major, 1 quartermaster sergeant, 1 drum major, 1 fife major
9 COMPANIES: EACH	1 captain, 1 captain lieutenant, 1 1st lieutenant, 3 2nd lieutenants, 65 enlisted men
TOTAL:	651 officers and men

On February 14, 1780 it had been announced that no more colonels of artillery would be made.

The actual tactical unit in the artillery was the individual gun crew. Ideally, a field gun had about 15 artillerists assigned to it; a heavy siege gun required more, a garrison piece fewer men.[41] Four field guns were supposed to be assigned to work with each infantry brigade. In addition to the usual supervising officers, it will be noticed that there were several grades of artillerists. A gunner supervised aiming the piece, a bombardier or fireworker checked the proper loading, and the lowly mattross muscled the piece around, rammed the charges home, and carried the ammunition. The term battery in those days meant a gun position and nothing more, and the idea of permanently attaching a particular group of men to a particular group of guns was not at all common at that time. An artillerist never knew from campaign to campaign what type ordnance he would serve. A gunner had to master all types, field and garrison; gun, howitzer, and mortar.

Even in the field, artillery was not very mobile. On the march, two to four rented horses were hitched to each field gun and ammunition wagon (more horses were used with heavy guns). Civilian teamsters drove the horses and the artillerymen marched beside them on foot. When action was imminent, the teamsters withdrew the horses to safety and the artillerists hauled the guns around using ropes and handspikes.

American artillerymen were armed with a miscellany of personal weapons—muskets and bayonets, musketoons, short sabers, or no proper weapons at all. Field guns were mostly brass 3 and 6 pounders of British manufacture, obsolescent French 4 pounders, and the prized Swedish-designed brass 4 pounders made in France. Iron guns and cannon cast in America were also used. Heavier weapons included 12, 18, and 24 pounder guns; 5.8 and 8 inch howitzers; and 8, 9, and 10 inch mortars. British materiel and gun drill were the models for the Americans.[42]

After June 17, 1783 all the artillery with the Main Army was formed into a battalion-size corps of reputedly two companies. The corps was commanded by Colonel Crane until November 3, 1783 when he was replaced by Major Bauman. On June 11, 1784 this was reduced to one company.

The American artillery came into its own rapidly during the war. Colonel (after January, 1777 brigadier general) Knox placed it on a solid footing and the battalions, although often below half of their authorized strength, showed considerable esprit d'corps. Nevertheless, the Revolution was not an artillerist's war. Artillery was essential for siege work, sometimes helpful in the field, but it was of secondary value to engineers in sieges and to the infantry in the open.

1st Battalion of Continental Artillery   The nucleus of this battalion was an artillery company under Captain Arundel that Congress authorized to be raised in Virginia on March 19, 1776.[43] On May 18, 1776 Congress voted to add 2 subalterns and 40 men to this company.[44] By November 26, 1776 this single company had been joined by a second one and on that date Congress voted to expand the Virginia companies into a regiment of 1 colonel, 1 lieutenant colonel, 1 major, and ten companies each of 1 captain, 3 lieutenants, 1 sergeant, 4 corporals, 8 gunners, 4 bombardiers, and 48 mattrosses.[45] January 8, 1778 it was recommended that two Maryland artillery companies be added to the battalion[46] and this was soon done. In 1781 the battalion was part of Virginia's quota. The battalion served with the Main Army from 1778 and later in the South. During 1782 attempts were made to merge the remnants of the 1st and 4th Battalions but rivalry among the officers of the two formations made this impossible.[47] The handful of men remained in the South until furloughed and discharged between June 11 and November 15, 1783.

COMMANDER: Colonel Charles Harrison November 30, 1776-June 17, 1783.

2nd Battalion of Continental Artillery This battalion was created on January 1, 1777 although existent Congressional records do not mention this. The battalion was most definitely always intended for Continental service. In the spring of 1777 it began to join the Main Army.[48] The companies came from New York and Connecticut. On January 8, 1778 this battalion was made up of four Connecticut companies (Jonathan Brown's, Lockwood's, Mansfield's, and Walker's)[49] and two New York companies (Bauman's and Doughty's).[50] Further companies were ordered raised to join this battalion—two in New Hampshire and one in Rhode Island.[51] Despite its heterogenous composition, the unit seems to have had considerable pride. It is known that this battalion had a band of music. Some men from this battalion served until the disbandment of the Main Army on November 5, 1783 when they were reassigned to Knox's tiny observation force in New York. When Knox's men were dismissed June 2, 1784, it was decided to retain Doughty's artillery company to guard the military stores at West Point and Fort Pitt. This company was subsequently incorporated into what is now the United States Army. Battery D of the 5th Artillery Regiment today claims to be the organizational descendent of Doughty's company.

COMMANDER: Colonel John Lamb January 1, 1777-June 17, 1783.

3rd Battalion of Continental Artillery This battalion was raised in Massachusetts over the winter of 1776-77 and detachments of it began to join the Main Army around April, 1777.[52] This battalion was perhaps the most homogenous in the Corps of Artillery. All twelve of its companies were from Massachusetts, at least until

Steven's Battalion was incorporated into it at the end of 1778. The battalion boasted a notable band of music.[53] The battalion served through the war, in 1781 being made part of the Massachusetts quota. Its last men probably left the army between June 17 and November 5, 1783 although a few may have stayed with Knox's little observation force until June 2, 1784.

COMMANDER: Colonel John Crane January 1, 1777-June 17, 1783. After this date Crane commanded the remnants of the Corps of Artillery until November 3, 1783.

4th Battalion of Continental Artillery   The 4th Battalion began as a Pennsylvania state unit, not a Continental one; Captain Proctor's Pennsylvania State Artillery Company. This company was present with the Flying Camp in 1776. In October, 1776 Proctor was made a major and directed to recruit a second company.[54] On January 29, 1777 the two state companies were with Washington's army as this seemed the place where they could do the most good in the defense of their state. A company of Continental infantry from the 2nd Pennsylvania Regiment was assigned to the guns with them. On January 31, an urgent plea from Washington secured the services of other Pennsylvania state artillerists from forts along the Delaware River. From this time until April, 1777 these requisitioned state troops along with two companies of New Jersey artillery (which see) were the only artillerists with the Main Army. As late as April the state was still trying to get its soldiers back, but a change in the military situation led to a change in heart and on June 20, 1777 the state artillery regiment was offered to the Continental Congress by whom it was accepted on July 19, 1777.[55] On January 8, 1778 the battalion was to be composed of nine Pennsylvania companies, two New Jersey companies (Clark's and Randall's), and a Maryland company (Lee's).[56] In 1778 the battalion had a band. Many in the regiment do not seem to have liked the Continental service. With its distinctive uniform, its tendency to still think of itself as the Pennsylvania State Regiment of Artillery, and its seniority-conscious commander, the battalion was a needle in the side of General Washington through the war. In 1781 the unit was placed in the Pennsylvania quota. The handful of men remaining in the battalion in 1783 were furloughed and discharged between June 11 and November 15 of that year.

COMMANDERS: Colonel Thomas Proctor Commission dated February 5, 1777-April 18, 1781.

Lieutenant Colonel Thomas Forest April, 1781-October 7, 1781.
Lieutenant Colonel Andrew Porter October, 1781-June 17, 1783.

Corps of Continental Light Dragoons The American mounted arm was variously referred to as light horse, horse, cavalry, or dragoons. Actually it was light dragoons. Light dragoons were intended to be mobile troops for scouting, raiding, screening, and pursuit. They were light enough in physique and equipment to perform their missions dismounted if necessary. They were not intended to charge formed troops.

The American Corps of Light Dragoons might be said to date from the autumn of 1777 when Count Pulaski was made a brigadier general in charge of cavalry. His command consisted of four regiments; 1st (Bland's), 2nd (Sheldon's), 3rd (Baylor's), and 4th (Moylan's). Only native Americans were to serve in the regiments.

Back on March 14, 1777 a uniform organization had been decreed for these regiments:

STAFF:	1 colonel, 1 lieutenant colonel, 1 major, 1 adjutant, 1 quartermaster, 1 paymaster, 1 surgeon, 1 surgeon's mate, 1 chaplain, 1 saddler, 1 riding master, 1 trumpet major, and 4 supernumeraries armed with sword and pistol
6 TROOPS: EACH	1 captain, 1 lieutenant, 1 cornet, 1 quartermaster sergeant, 1 orderly or drill sergeant, 4 corporals, 1 trumpeter, 1 farrier, 1 armorer, 32 privates
TOTAL:	280 officers and men

Brigadier General Pulaski was authorized a brigade major (subinspector) and a chaplain to staff the corps and after May 27, 1778, a quartermaster as well.

On May 27, 1778 the organization of a "cavalry battalion" was changed to:

STAFF:	1 colonel, 1 lieutenant colonel, 1 major, 1 surgeon, 1 surgeon's mate, 1 riding master, 1 saddler, 1 trumpet major
6 TROOPS: EACH	1 captain, 2 lieutenants, 1 cornet, 1 quartermaster sergeant, 2 sergeants, 5 corporals, 1 trumpeter, 1 farrier, 54 privates
TOTAL:	416 officers and men

27

Three lieutenants did double duty as adjutant, quartermaster, and paymaster.

Actually Pulaski's brigade was pretty much of a farce. The various regiments had only 120-150 men apiece in reality,[57] and simply could not be concentrated owing to their haphazard logistical base. In all fairness to Pulaski, getting horses, fodder, recruits, and special equipment would have been difficult for even the greatest administrative executive in the world. Pulaski was not the man for the job, however. He was dashing, moody, and had difficulty with American language and customs. He was no desk general at all. After March, 1778 Pulaski got himself transferred to an independent command and after May 27, 1779 any pretext of a cavalry brigade was given up[58] although one finds mention of the Corps of Light Dragoons afterwards in the context of the whole of the mounted branch of service. In August, 1780 an inspector and sub-inspector were authorized for the cavalry, but no overall commander.

In both the British and the Continental Armies of the Revolution, fighting on foot was often necessary for the light dragoons. There were never enough horses available to mount whole regiments. The mixed horse and foot units resulting, of necessity, were styled legions, in the vernacular of the times. Owing to the often difficult terrain, the legion was found to be a valuable type of formation for scouting and harassing the enemy. Also cavalry needed infantry protection for its bases. Accordingly there was no great haste to procure expensive horses for completely mounted regiments.

On February 14, 1780 it was announced no more colonels of cavalry would be made.[59] Effective January 1, 1781 the last change in mounted organization went into effect. This converted the light dragoons to legionary corps, each consisting of:

STAFF:	1 colonel, 1 lieutenant colonel, 1 major, 1 adjutant, 1 quartermaster, 1 paymaster, 1 surgeon, 1 surgeon's mate, 1 riding master, 1 saddler, 1 trumpet major
4 MOUNTED: TROOPS EACH	1 captain, 2 lieutenants, 1 cornet, 1 quartermaster sergeant, 2 sergeants, 5 corporals, 1 trumpeter, 1 farrier, 60 privates

2 dismounted troops of similar organization to the mounted ones. It is said the foot dragoons had drummers in lieu of trumpeters.

TOTAL:	455 officers and men

Washington's draft of the General Order says 6 mounted and 2 dismounted troops,[60] but most other contemporary copies of the 1781 reorganization plan give the 4 mounted and 2 dismounted troops quoted above.

American light dragoons were variously armed. Ideally all troopers, sergeants, and corporals should have had a sword, carbine or musketoon, and a pair of pistols. Trumpeters were to have swords only and officers were to carry swords and a pair of psitols. All were to have a helmet of some type. Actual armament varied. The sword and helmet were usually obtained, but firearms were in short supply.

It seems fair to say that American horsemanship, while not outstanding, was equal to that of the British and that in the last years of the war there were competent Continental troopers. Under bold and efficient Lieutenant Colonel William Washington, Continental dragoons put their British and American Loyalist adversaries to shame. Of all arms, however, cavalry was hardest for Americans to produce. It was expensive and it took a long time for officers and soldiers on horseback to develop into cavalry leaders and effective troopers. No American dragoon regiment ever produced much over 300 men or 150 horses.

1st Regiment of Continental Light Dragoons   During 1776 a number of troops of light dragoons composed of gentlemen volunteers were sanctioned by the Virginia government. Formed into a squadron under Theodoric Bland, they were offered to Congress in November, 1776 and subsequently accepted on January 14, 1777.[61] The squadron was later designated the 1st Regiment in the Corps of Light Dragoons. In 1778 the regiment's recruiting and supply area was to be limited to the area south of the James River.[62] By 1780 the regiment had become so understrength that its remaining men were mixed with those of the 3rd Regiment of Light Dragoons, while most of their officers were sent back to Virginia to recruit. In 1781 the regiment was redesignated the 1st Legionary Corps and assigned to Virginia's quota. In 1781 the regiment was able to enlist only 60 recruits, these serving in the Yorktown campaign with the "Light Corps".[63] By November 9, 1782 if not months earlier, the men of the 1st Legionary Corps were amalgamated with those of the 3rd. The last men of this corps were probably furloughed out between June 12, 1783 and September of that year.

2nd Regiment of Continental Light Dragoons

COMMANDERS: Colonel Theodoric Bland Commissioned March 31, 1777-December 10, 1779.
Colonel Anthony W. White February 16, 1780-November 9, 1782.

2nd Regiment of Continental Light Dragoons On December 12, 1776 Congress appointed Elisha Sheldon of Connecticut to raise a regiment of light horse.[64] General Washington instructed him on December 16 to organize his regiment as 1 lieutenant colonel commandant, 1 major, 1 adjutant, 1 surgeon, 1 surgeon's mate, and six troops each of 1 captain, 1 lieutenant, 1 cornet, 1 quartermaster, 2 sergeants, 2 corporals, 1 trumpeter, 1 farrier, and 34 privates. In 1778 the regimental recruiting area was to be the area east of the North River.[65] In January, 1781 the regiment was renamed the 2nd Legionary Corps and assigned to the Connecticut quota. On June 9, 1783 the 2nd Legionary Corps was furloughed for fourteen months and in consequence of its discharge effective November 5, 1783, the regiment never mustered again.[66]

COMMANDER: Colonel Elisha Sheldon December 12, 1776-November 5, 1783.

3rd Regiment of Continental Light Dragoons January 9, 1777, George Baylor was appointed a colonel for a regiment of light dragoons he was supposed to raise. One modern historian states the regiment was sometimes called the Lady Washington Dragoons, but contemporary evidence of this nickname is lacking. General Washington certainly knew many of the regiment's officers and he looked after his friends as well as he could. In 1778 the regiment was assigned the area between the Susquehanna and the James Rivers for future recruiting.[67] Most of the regiment were Virginians, but Pennsylvanians allegedly made up most of one troop, and another troop had a large number of Marylanders. On the night of September 27, 1778 the regiment was surprised in billets at Tappan, New York. Of 104 men in the regiment, only a score or so escaped either bloody massacre or capture. Baylor himself was shot through the lungs and captured, but was subsequently exchanged and the regiment reraised. Owing to Baylor's condition, Lieutenant Colonel William Washington assumed command of the regiment in the field. In 1780 the regiment suffered further grave losses in the Carolinas. Attempts to recruit in North Carolina netted few men so following the Battle of Camden in August, 1780 the remaining enlisted men in the 1st and 4th Light Dragoon detachments in the South were turned over to Colonel Washington's command and the combined 1st, 3rd, and 4th Regiments formed into four troops who served with great distinction at the Cowpens and Guilford Courthouse.[68] In 1781 the regiment was redesignated the 3rd Legionary Corps and assigned to the Virginia quota, but few recruits came in. By November 9, 1782 the recruits of the 1st Legionary Corps were added to Colonel Washington's unit bringing it up to five troops. The men were furloughed between June 12 and September of 1783 and subsequently discharged.

    COMMANDER: Colonel George Baylor January 9, 1777-November 15, 1783.

4th Regiment of Continental Light Dragoons   In January, 1777, Stephen Moylan of Pennsylvania was commissioned by Congress to raise a regiment of light dragoons of which he was to be colonel. The regiment consisted mainly of Pennsylvanians, but there were a small number of Marylanders. In 1778 the regiment was assigned the area between the North River and the Susquehanna for recruiting and purchasing. The regiment does not seem to have been too heavily engaged until 1780 when part of it was sent south where it suffered numerous casualties. Like the 3rd Regiment, the 4th Light Dragoons also tried to recruit in North Carolina, but with little success and, after Camden, the enlisted men from the regiment were taken into Colonel Washington's mixed command.[69] In 1781 the regiment was renamed the 4th Legionary Corps and assigned to Pennsylvania's quota. A number of new mounted recruits were apparently sent south to participate in the Yorktown campaign, but on June 13, 1782 the remaining mounted men of the corps were all assigned to the mixed command of Colonel Washington.[70] Around December 15, 1782 the remaining elements from this regiment were disbanded, the infantry company of the corps going into the infantry of the Pennsylvania Line, but retaining its higher legionary corps pay.[71]

    COMMANDER: Colonel Stephen Moylan January 5, 1777-December, 1782.

Continental Line   After about 1777 one usually finds the infantry regiments of the Continental Army referred to as the Continental Line, thus implying these regiments would form a line of battle in defense of the thirteen rebel colonies of the continent. This is what is normally meant by the term Continental Line. The states' contingents of infantry which would compose this line were often referred to individually as the Massachusetts Line or the North Carolina Line, etc. Promotions were determined by seniority within one's state contingent rather than within the Continental Line as a whole.

This term "Continental Line" was rather loosely used, however, for in some correspondence, not just infantry, but cavalry and artillery of a state's contingent are also referred to as part of the Continental Line or one of its segments. Also the term "State Line" was also used to describe the state's contingent to the Continental Line. Unfortunately the term "State Line" was also used to distinguish state troops (which see) from Continentals so it is not always clear what is meant when one runs across designations like "Pennsylvania State Line" or "Line of this state" in old records.

1st Continental Regiment   *See* Pennsylvania Rifle Regiment.

2nd Continental Regiment   This New Hampshire regiment served from the beginning of 1776 until the reorganization of the New Hampshire Continental troops after November 8, 1776.
> COMMANDERS: Colonel James Reed January 1, 1776-August 9, 1776.
> Lieutenant Colonel Israel Gilman August, 1776-December 31, 1776.

3rd Continental Regiment   The 3rd was a Massachusetts regiment. Served from January to December of 1776.
> COMMANDER: Colonel Ebenezer Learned January 1, 1776-December 31, 1776.

4th Continental Regiment   The 4th was a Massachusetts regiment. Served from January to December, 1776.
> COMMANDERS: Colonel John Nixon January 1, 1776-August 9, 1776.
> Colonel Thomas Nixon August 9, 1776-December 31, 1776.

5th Continental Regiment   Another New Hampshire regiment that served from the beginning of 1776 until the reorganization of the state's Continentals after November 8, 1776.
> COMMANDER: Colonel John Stark January 1, 1776-December 31, 1776.

6th Continental Regiment   A Massachusetts regiment. Served from January to December, 1776.
COMMANDER: Colonel Asa Whitcomb January 1, 1776-December 31, 1776.

7th Continental Regiment   Massachusetts regiment. Served from January to December, 1776.
COMMANDER: Colonel William Prescott January 1, 1776-December 31, 1776.

8th Continental Regiment   A regiment of New Hampshire men that served from the beginning of 1776 until the reorganization of the state's Continentals after November 8, 1776.
COMMANDER: Colonel Enoch Poor January 1, 1776-December 31, 1776.

9th Continental Regiment   This regiment of Rhode Islanders served officially from January through December of 1776.
COMMANDER: Colonel James Varnum January 1, 1776-December 31, 1776.

10th Continental Regiment   The regiment was formed of Connecticut men at the end of 1775 and served from January 1, 1776 to the end of the year when the men returned home.
COMMANDERS: Colonel Samuel Parsons January 1, 1776-August 9, 1776.
Colonel John Tyler August 10, 1776-December 31, 1776.

11th Continental Regiment   This regiment of Rhode Islanders served officially from January to December of 1776.
COMMANDER: Colonel Daniel Hitchcock January 1, 1776-December 31, 1776.

12th Continental Regiment   Massachusetts regiment. Served January to December, 1776.
COMMANDER: Colonel Moses Little January 1, 1776-December 31, 1776.

13th Continental Regiment   Massachusetts regiment. Served January to December, 1776.

COMMANDER: Colonel Joseph Reed January 1, 1776-December 31, 1776.

14th Continental Regiment   Better known as Glover's Marblehead Regiment, this Massachusetts regiment is perhaps the most colorful and famous of the twenty-seven Continental regiments of 1776. There were sailors in other regiments from New England as well as in this one, but this regiment seems to have been mostly sailors and fishermen. This well-drilled regiment stayed with Washington's army after most of the Massachusetts men had gone home and in view of the regiment's composition, it was selected to ferry the army across the icy Delaware River on Christmas Eve, 1776. This it did in fine fashion, earning the regiment a place in the history books of future generations. The regiment's similar performance earlier in the Long Island campaign is often overlooked. The regiment was disbanded in January, 1777.

COMMANDER: Colonel John Glover January 1, 1776-December 31, 1776.

15th Continental Regiment   Massachusetts regiment. Served January to December, 1776.

COMMANDER: Colonel John Paterson January 1, 1776-December 31, 1776.

16th Continental Regiment   Massachusetts regiment. Served January to December, 1776.

COMMANDER: Colonel Paul Sargent January 1, 1776-December 31, 1776.

17th Continental Regiment   A Connecticut regiment that served from January 1, 1776 to the end of the year.

COMMANDER: Colonel Jedediah Huntington January 1, 1776-December 31, 1776.

18th Continental Regiment   Massachusetts regiment. Served January to December, 1776.

COMMANDER: Colonel Edmund Phinney January 1, 1776-December 31, 1776.

19th Continental Regiment   A Connecticut regiment. It served from January 1, 1776 until sometime in February, 1777 as the men had been persuaded to extend their enlistments for six weeks during this period of emergency.[72]

COMMANDER: Colonel Charles Webb January 1, 1776-December 31, 1776.

20th Continental Regiment   This Connecticut regiment had an organizational history identical to the 19th Continental Regiment (which see).

COMMANDERS: Colonel Benedict Arnold January 1, 1776-January 10, 1776.
Lieutenant Colonel John Durkee January 10, 1776-December 31, 1776. Durkee was promoted to colonel on August 12, 1776.

21st Continental Regiment   Massachusetts Regiment. Served January to December, 1776.

COMMANDER: Colonel Jonathan Ward January 1, 1776-December 31, 1776.

22nd Continental Regiment   A Connecticut regiment that served from January 1, 1776 until the end of the year.

COMMANDER: Colonel Samuel Wyllys January 1, 1776-December 31, 1776.

23rd Continental Regiment   Massachusetts regiment. Served January to December, 1776.

COMMANDER: Colonel John Bailey January 1, 1776-December 31, 1776.

24th Continental Regiment   Massachusetts regiment. Served January to December, 1776.

COMMANDER: Colonel John Greaton January 1, 1776-December 31, 1776.

25th Continental Regiment   Massachusetts regiment. Served January to December, 1776.

COMMANDERS: Colonel William Bond January 1, 1776-August 31, 1776.
Lieutenant Colonel Ichabod Alden September, 1776-December 31, 1776.

26th Continental Regiment   Massachusetts regiment. Served January
to December, 1776.
COMMANDER: Colonel Loammi Baldwin January 1, 1776-
December 31, 1776.

27th Continental Regiment   Massachusetts regiment. Served January
to December, 1776.
COMMANDER: Colonel Israel Hutchinson January 1, 1776-
December 31, 1776.

D

Dearborn's Light Infantry Battalion   In the summer of 1777 a body of light infantry, 300 strong, was picked from the regiments of the Main Army. The corps was attached to Morgan's Rifle Corps (which see) and presumably consisted of men with similar qualifications, but armed with muskets and bayonets rather than rifles. The corps was broken up over the winter of 1777-78.

    COMMANDER: Major Henry Dearborn (promoted to lieutenant colonel on September 19, 1777).

Delaware Regiment   On December 9, 1775 Congress authorized a Delaware battalion and in January, 1776 Colonel Haslet's Delaware Regiment was accordingly accepted into the Continental service.[73] Haslet's Regiment served with distinction through the year. Haslet, himself, was killed at Princeton, but under his successor, Colonel David Hall and a cadre of Haslet's former officers, the regiment was rerecruited and reorganized for the 1777 campaign. Through the years Hall's Delaware Regiment maintained its reputation. Although in 1776 the entire regiment wore the cap associated with light infantry, the author has yet to find any contemporary evidence the whole unit was intended for that role. There is reason to believe, however, that in 1776 and 1777, before all Continental battalions had light infantry companies, that the Delaware Regiment did have one of its companies trained in that capacity.

The disaster at Camden on August 16, 1780 shattered this famous regiment. Most of the regiment's men were killed or captured in that battle. Afterwards, the survivors formed two companies under Captain Kirkwood[74] and were assigned to a mixed Maryland-Delaware Light Infantry Battalion (which see) after October 30, 1780.[75] At Guilford Courthouse on March 15, 1781, the Delaware men formed a flank detachment for the front line and suffered further casualties. By late 1781 a few recruits arrived to strengthen the tiny remnant of the old Delaware Regiment to 4 companies. On June 13, 1782 General Greene assigned the regiment to Lieutenant Colonel Lauren's Light Infantry Corps.[76] The Delaware men were furloughed soon after June 11, 1783.

COMMANDERS: Colonel John Haslet Continental commission dated January 19, 1776-January 3, 1777.
Colonel David Hall April 5, 1777-May 17, 1782. In 1780 Lieutenant Colonel Joseph Vaughan was in actual command of the regiment until he was captured at Camden.

Captain Dorsey's Maryland Artillery Company   Together with Brown's company (which see) Dorsey's company was taken over from the state, where it had originated in 1776, by Congress. It also was assigned to the 1st Continental Artillery Battalion. On September 3, 1779 Brown's company merged with Dorsey's Most of the company was captured at Camden on August 16, 1780. On January 1, 1781 a lack of manpower caused the company to be ordered broken up and its personnel to be assigned to other companies.[77]

COMMANDER: Captain Richard Dorsey Artillery commission dated May 4, 1777.

Captain Doughty's Independent Artillery Company   On March 1, 1776 Captain Doughty was appointed to command a company of artillery to be raised in New Jersey. When the unit became Continental is not mentioned. On January 1, 1777 Doughty and perhaps a few of his old company were taken into Lamb's Battalion of Continental Artillery (the 2nd) and apparently sent to New York to raise men as later mentions of the 2nd Battalion indicate Doughty's company was from New York.

COMMANDER: Captain John Doughty

Captain John Doyle's Independent Company   A Pennsylvania company raised July 6, 1776 although it is not certain that it entered the Continental service at that time. For a time it was attached to Malcolm's Additional Continental Regiment (which see). Eventually it was incorporated into the 11th Pennsylvania Regiment on January 13, 1779.[78]

Major Jeremiah Dugan's Corps of Rangers   Dugan was appointed lieutenant colonel of a body of rangers totalling three companies each of 1 captain, 2 lieutenants, and 100 men, by Congress on March 28, 1776.[79] There is some question if the corps was ever raised.

Captain Robert Durkee's Independent Company   This may have been one of the three independent companies that Congress allowed Connecticut to raise at Continental expense by resolve of June 24, 1776 to garrison the New London area. At any rate, Durkee's commission was dated August 26, 1776 and his company was raised in the Wyoming area. The company was sent to join the Main Army around January 1, 1777 and saw considerable service. The company was consolidated with Ransom's company on June 23, 1778 to form Spaulding's Company (which see).[80]

E

Eastern Department   This department came into its own in 1777. It included the civilized sections of the New England states.

Colonel Elmore's Connecticut Regiment   In April, 1776 this regiment was brought into existence at the request of Congress. It served in the Northern Department until its one year enlistment ran out in 1777. Most of its men then joined the Connecticut, Massachusetts, or New York Lines.[81]

    COMMANDER: Colonel Samuel Elmore April 15, 1776-April, 1777.

Engineer's Department   On June 16, 1775 it was decided that a chief engineer with two assistants should be appointed for the Continental Army. In those days engineers were very specially educated men and always held a gentlemanly status in armies, if no military rank. Enlisted men working with them were never called engineers, in contrast to modern parlance. On March 28, 1776 two more engineers were to be appointed to serve in the Southern Department.[82] The number of qualified American engineers was very tiny and most of the engineers commissioned were volunteers from the French Army. Early in 1778 Washington proposed that three companies of workmen, each of 1 captain, 3 lieutenants, 4 sergeants, 4 corporals, and 60 privates, be raised to assist the engineers,[83] but not until June of that year was the Corps of Sappers and Miners authorized.[84] The Corps of Sappers and Miners was to consist of three companies each of 1 captain, 3 lieutenants, 4 sergeants, 4 corporals, 1 drummer, 1 fifer, and 50 privates. Most of the sappers and miners were men detached from Connecticut and Massachusetts infantry regiments to serve as long as required by the engineers to whom they were attached to build fortifications or dig saps (mines) for sieges. Most of the engineers, sappers and miners were furloughed between May 18, 1783 and September 26 of that year.[85]

F

Flower's Regiment of Artillery Artificers *See* Regiment of Artillery Artificers.

The Flying Camp In July, 1776 a flying camp (mobile reserve) was created by Congress in the middle colonies. It was composed mostly of militia and state troops from Maryland, Pennsylvania, and Delaware. The men were to be considered in the service of Congress and were to be paid with Congressional funds. State troops were probably much better organized than the militia and some of them were ordered north to reenforce Washington's army after the British began to land. These state units were paid as and served with the Continental Army and during the reorganization of late 1776 and early 1777 their men were largely incorporated into the Continental Army. Important state units at the camp included Smallwood's Maryland Regiment (which see), several Maryland independent infantry companies (see 2nd Maryland Regiment), Colonel Miles' Pennsylvania State Rifle Regiment of two battalions each of 6 companies, Colonel Atlee's Pennsylvania State Musketry Battalion of eight companies, and Captain Proctor's Pennsylvania State Artillery Company (see 4th Battalion of Continental Artillery).

Colonel Forman's Additional Continental Regiment   Colonel Forman was issued his commission as colonel of an additional regiment on January 12, 1777. This regiment seems to have been raised mostly in New Jersey and Maryland. On July 1, 1778 its enlisted men were incorporated into the New Jersey Line and on August 8, 1779 its officers with what new recruits they had gathered were merged with Spencer's Additional Regiment (which see).[86]

COMMANDER: Colonel David Forman

Frederick Detachment   During 1781 and 1782 the remnants of the old so called "Maryland Corps" (which see) served at Frederick as a prisoner of war guard. The detachment was of about company strength.[87] In 1782-83 there is mention of a company-size Frederick German Artillery.

Free and Independent Chasseurs   *See* Armand's Legion.

French Regiment   In January, 1778 a letter was received by the Virginia state government from John Marie Bory offering to import a regiment from the French West Indies for the state.[88] No regiment was ever brought, however, although there was a French Company in the Virginia service.

G

Generals' Staffs   George Washington was general and commander-in-chief of the Continental Congress's forces during the war. Under him were major generals in charge of separate armies and divisions and brigadier generals in charge of brigades. The staffs of these general officers were reasonably small. The modern staff system had not yet come into being and a commander was pretty much on his own when it came to formulating battle plans, especially in the Continental Army. In addition to the heads of the various staff departments (see Staff Departments) each general had at least one aide and sometimes a clerk. On June 16, 1775 the commander of the Continental Army was authorized 3 aides and a secretary; the commander of the Separate Army, one secretary.[89] By 1777 General Washington had 6 aides.

Georgia Light Horse   By mid-1776 some of the mounted freebooters who rampaged the Florida frontier were requisitioned temporarily into the Continental Army by the local commander. Several companies of light horse had previously been created among these frontiersmen by the state—on paper. The legislation by Congress of July 24, 1776 to form a regiment of rangers in Georgia on the same organizational plan as the South Carolina Rangers (see 3rd South Carolina Regiment) was no more effective than earlier state legislation.[90] At best the Georgia Light Horse were vigilantes; at worst, bandits. They served when and where their ringleader-officers could persuade them to and they had more stomach for plunder than for fighting. On February 13, 1778 Congress reduced the "regiment" to four independent companies each of 50 men,[91] but no one in Georgia paid the slightest attention to this—the light horse at one time flatly refusing to present themselves for service and as they had never received any pay at all, it is little wonder.[92] On February 11, 1780 Georgia's quota of Continental troops was to include a regiment of horsemen,[93] but this was never raised.

Georgia Rangers   *See* Georgia Light Horse.

1st Georgia Regiment   On November 4, 1775 the Continental Congress authorized a battalion of foot soldiers to be raised in Georgia at Continental expense. Officers were appointed that December. On February 16, 1776 the Georgia Battalion began organizing. It was to have 1 colonel, 1 lieutenant colonel, 1 major, and eight companies including a rifle company. Each company was to have 1 captain, 2 lieutenants, 1 ensign, 4 sergeants, 4 corporals, 1 drummer, and at least 48 privates. Even this small unit was more than could be raised in the sparsely populated colony. In April the colonel reported his regiment was understrength and that only 10 riflemen had been found. He asked for more men to defend Georgia.[94] The regiment soon lost many of its men to desertion, disease, and enemy action, but elements of it served on until 1779 and 1780 when the last of the Georgia Line—six officers without men—were captured at Charleston on May 12, 1780.

> COMMANDERS: Colonel Lachlan McIntosh January 7, 1776-September 16, 1776.
> Colonel Joseph Habersham September 16, 1776-March 21, 1778.
> Colonel Robert Rae March 21, 1778-?

1st Georgia Battalion   In the late spring of 1782 the situation in Georgia had improved enough for Georgia to re-form the infantry battalion called for by its Continental quota. Officers for this unit had been elected as early as January in anticipation of this improved situation and by July 29, 1782 the corps was organizing. The battalion was to have both line and light infantry companies and also about two troops of cavalry each of 1 captain, 1 lieutenant, 1 cornet, 1 quartermaster sergeant, 3 sergeants, 4 corporals, 2 trumpeters, and 64 privates.[95] By late 1782, the battalion had reached a strength of 150 men.[96] These were furloughed according to prior Congressional resolution in late July, 1783 and subsequently discharged.[97]

2nd Georgia Regiment   On July 5, 1776 Congress authorized two additional battalions, including one of riflemen to be raised in the Carolinas and Virginia and sent to defend Georgia. Service was obscurely referred to as the same terms as other Continental units, but Congress had just authorized its first three year units, so it is difficult to tell whether the new Georgia battalions were to serve the usual one year (the common interpretation) or the new three year hitch.[98] At any rate, Georgia appointed the officers for the 2nd and 3rd Georgia Regiments and recruiting began. This "recruiting campaign" was a fiasco. The recruiting officers went about their business without much zeal and most of the men they signed up promptly jumped bounty and deserted. The host states complained that the Georgians disrupted the recruiting of their own units. Only a handful of men ever marched south into the state they were to defend. February 13, 1778, the Georgia infantry regiments were cut from four to two by Congress,[99] but this legislation went unheeded and the four battalions continued to exist until November 28, 1779 when the state government decided to merge the four miserable units totalling under 200 men into one battalion.[100] This was approved by Congress, but by then the British forces were in Georgia in strength and the capture of the last six Georgia officers at Charleston in 1780 spelled the end of the Georgia Continentals till 1782.

COMMANDER: Colonel Samuel Elbert July 5, 1776-?

3rd Georgia Regiment   This unit was authorized at the same time as the 2nd Georgia Regiment of July 5, 1776 and its record and fate was identical to that unit. *(See* 2nd Georgia Regiment.)

COMMANDERS: Colonel James Screven July 5, 1776-March 20, 1778.
Colonel John Stirk March 20, 1778-?

4th Georgia Regiment   This regiment was apparently created sometime late in 1776 and was intended to recruit in the Carolinas and

Virginia. Its record and fate were similar to the 2nd Georgia Regiment (which see).
COMMANDER: Colonel John White February 1, 1777-?

Georgia Riflemen   On April 4, 1782 General Wayne requisitioned 200 Georgia riflemen to serve Congress for two months.[101] It is debatable whether this unit should be considered Continental.

German Battalion   Following the recommendation of the previous month, Congress on June 27, 1776 authorized the German Battalion of four Pennsylvania and four Maryland companies to be raised among the German settlers in those colonies. The men were to be enlisted for three years—some of the first men to be so enlisted.[102] On July 17, another company was added.[103] On February 26, 1778 the German Battalion was officially made a part of Maryland's quota to facilitate supply and recruitment.[104] The unit was numbered as the 8th Maryland, but was usually still referred to as the German Battalion. The battalion formed the nucleus of the Maryland Corps (which see) which also contained men from the rest of the Maryland Line and Rawlings' corps. Effective January 1, 1781 the battalion was broken up, most of its men going into Hazen's Regiment. *(See* 2nd Canadian Regiment). The rest of the men were retained in the Frederick Detachment (which see) of the Maryland Line.
COMMANDERS: Colonel Nicholas Haussegger June, 1776-March 19, 1777.
Colonel the Baron De Arendt March 19, 1777-January 1, 1781.

German Volunteer Corps   This unit of German deserters was drafted in July, 1779 into Armand's corps with other foreign recruits before it was ever completed.[105]

General Gist's Light Corps   On June 13, 1782 General Greene formed a light corps in his army under General Gist. The corps consisted of Colonel Baylor's Cavalry—3rd and 4th Light Dragoons, cavalry of Lee's Legion—and also Lieutenant Colonel Laurens' Light Infantry—dismounted troopers of 3rd Light Dragoons, Delaware Regiment, infantry of Lee's Legion, 100 picked men from other units under Major Beall.
Lieutenant Colonel Laurens was a South Carolinian, but his

command was largely Virginians.[106] Laurens was killed August 27, 1782 and replaced by Major James Hamilton. The corps apparently broke up in 1783.

Colonel Gist's Ranger Corps   On January 11, 1777 Washington authorized Colonel Nathaniel Gist to raise a Continental corps consisting of four companies of rangers. Two companies of Gist's corps were raised in Maryland,[107] the rest in Virginia. On January 1, 1779 Thurston's Additional Regiment merged with Gist's, and on April 22 of that year, Grayson's Regiment followed suit. Very little else is mentioned about this unit. It was apparently considered as one of the sixteen additional regiments of infantry and whether it was actually employed as rangers is difficult to tell. The regiment was disbanded by General Order of November 1, 1780; this order effective as of January 1, 1781.

COMMANDER: Colonel Nathaniel Gist January 11, 1777-captured at Charleston May 12, 1780.

Colonel Grayson's Additional Continental Regiment   Grayson was commissioned to raise an additional regiment on January 11, 1777. Two or three of its companies were raised in Maryland, most of the rest in Virginia.[108] On April 22, 1779 this unit was merged into Gist's Ranger Corps (which see).

COMMANDER: Colonel William Grayson

Green Mountain Boys   Also called Green Mountain Rangers. Originally the frontiersmen of Ethan Allen's patriotic gang. *See* Warner's Continental Regiment.

Colonel Gridley's Massachusetts Artillery Regiment   This regiment was taken into the Continental Army at the end of July, 1775. Its strength was set at 1 colonel, 1 lieutenant colonel, 2 majors, and six companies. Gridley's regiment served until its enlistments ran out toward the end of the year and it was reorganized for 1776 by Colonel Knox, using many of Gridley's old personnel. *See* Knox's Artillery Regiment.

COMMANDER: Colonel Richard Gridley

H

Captain Alexander Hamilton's New York Artillery Company   Raised
in the spring of 1776 as a state company. The exact date when it entered the Continental service is not mentioned. Served at Trenton in
December, 1776 and subsequently some of the men were absorbed
into Colonel Lamb's 2nd Continental Battalion of Artillery *(see*
2nd Battalion of Continental Artillery).

> COMMANDER: Captain Alexander Hamilton State commis-
> sion dated March 14, 1776; became aide de
> camp to Washington March 1, 1777.

Colonel Hartley's Additional Continental Regiment   Thomas Hartley
was appointed colonel of an additional Continental regiment on
January 1, 1777. The regiment seems to have recruited in Pennsylvania and Maryland. His regiment picked up the nickname of Foot
Guards, somehow, although there was nothing of distinction about
the regiment. On January 13, 1779 Hartley's Regiment merged
with Patton's and four Pennsylvania independent companies to
form the new 11th Pennsylvania Regiment.[109]

> COMMANDER: Colonel Thomas Hartley

Colonel Heard's Minutemen   Actually not a Continental unit, but a
picked body of militiamen who were tendered some pay for their
services on Long Island by Congress on March 30, 1776.[110]

Colonel Henley's Additional Continental Regiment   David Henley was empowered to raise a regiment on January 1, 1777. Most of the regiment was from Massachusetts. Ordered consolidated with Jackson's Additional Continental Regiment (which see) on April 22, 1779.

COMMANDER: Colonel David Henley

Lieutenant Colonel Daniel Horry's Dragoons   On February 24, 1779 Colonel Daniel Horry was appointed to raise a regiment of light dragoons by the South Carolina government.[111] The regiment was actually never taken into the Continental service, but it served alongside the Continental forces and after its surrender at Charleston on May 12, 1780, it was mentioned among the Continental troops of South Carolina.[112] The regiment was to have had seven or eight troops.

Lieutenant Colonel Peter Horry's South Carolina Regiment   General Greene allowed Peter Horry, one of Francis Marion's officers, to raise a Continental regiment in South Carolina sometime in mid-1781. This regiment was a creation of emergency. It was partly light dragoons and partly infantry. On September 24, 1781 the regiment was described as having many men,[113] but on December 24 the regiment had not yet been taken into the Continental Army.[114] The next year Horry became involved in a bitter dispute with another unit commander, Mayham, over rank, and in consequence of this dispute, the Tory forces were able to surprise and disperse both Horry's and Mayham's uncooperative commands in February, 1782. On March 12, 1782 General Greene and the governor of South Carolina decided that the remnants of Horry's regiment should be incorporated into Mayham's Legion (which see).[115] Some time after March 29 this was done and the men became state troops.[116]

Major Hyde's Connecticut Light Horse   Possibly this was the one or more troops of light horse raised in the vicinity of Albany by General Schuyler prior to May 27, 1777.[117] The corps served in the Saratoga campaign, Hyde, himself, being wounded. There is little information on this body regarding its length of service or even confirmation of its Continental status.

COMMANDER: Major Elijah Hyde

I

Infantry Organization   Infantry—infantry of the line, or line infantry—comprised the bulk of the Continental Army. Infantry, as opposed to light infantry (see Corps of Light Infantry), fought in close formation, firing volleys in the general direction of the enemy at its officers' commands.

The normal tactical unit of the infantry was the battalion. The administrative unit was the regiment. These terms were often used interchangeably, but sometimes not. A battalion was the smallest unit of men that manuevered and fought together. Usually a battalion was divided into four divisions (sometimes called grand divisions), each of two platoons (sometimes called divisions). The divisions and platoons were to facilitate fire control and existed only within a battalion in formation as they were not permanent subdivisions.

The regiment was the instrument through which men were recruited and supplies distributed. The subdivision of the regiment was the company.

It was usual for each regiment to form one battalion, but one sometimes finds regiments so small that the effective men from two or more of them had to be pooled to form a battalion. On rare occasions the opposite occurred and a strong regiment might form two battalions. In 1778 Von Steuben's regulations split a regiment of over 320 musketeers into two battalions and specified that no battalion was to have under 160 musketeers.

Infantry Organization

The army of 1775 had a hodgepodge of different regimental organizations. After about October 9, 1775, there was some attempt at standardizing regimental or battalion organization. This resulted in two slightly different battalion organizations. The "October style" battalions each had:

STAFF: 1 colonel, 1 lieutenant colonel, 1 major, 1 adjutant, and (after December 1) 1 surgeon

8 COMPANIES: 1 captain, 1 lieutenant, 1 ensign, 4 sergeants, EACH   68 privates

TOTAL: 605 officers and men

This was the organization originally intended for the New Jersey, Pennsylvania, and Delaware battalions, but by the end of the year it was apparently losing ground to the table of organization authorized for the army around Boston on November 4, 1775. The "November style" battalions were to have:

STAFF: 1 colonel, 1 lieutenant colonel, 1 major, 1 adjutant, 1 quartermaster, 1 surgeon, 1 surgeon's mate, 1 chaplain

8 COMPANIES: 1 captain, 2 lieutenants, 1 ensign, 4 sergeants, EACH   4 corporals, 1 drummer, 1 fifer, 76 privates

TOTAL: 728 officers and men

This battalion organization was adopted for the 27 Continental regiments, Bedel's New Hampshire Rangers, the Virginia regiments, the North Carolinians, the Delawares, and possibly the New Jersey battalions. On March 30, 1776 all regiments were allowed a surgeon's mate.[118] In July, 1776 1 paymaster, 1 sergeant major, 1 quartermaster sergeant, 1 drum major, and 1 fife major were authorized for each battalion.

On May 27, 1778 Congress adopted a new organization for infantry regiments.

STAFF: 1 surgeon, 1 surgeon's mate, 1 sergeant major, 1 quartermaster sergeant, 1 drum major, 1 fife major

8 LINE OR: 1 company commander, 1 lieutenant, 1 ensign, 3 sergeants, 3 corporals, 1 drummer, 1 fifer, 53 privates
BATTALION
COMPANIES
EACH

1 light company organized like a line company. The light company was usually detached to the Corps of Light Infantry.

TOTAL: 582 officers and men

The company commanders were, in fact, the colonel, the lieutenant colonel, the major, and six captains. The lieutenant of the colonel's company was called a captain lieutenant. Because the three senior officers did double duty as did three lieutenants who acted as adjutant, quartermaster, and paymaster, it was possible to reduce the number of expensive officers' salaries. In the interest of economy, it was further announced on that date that no more colonels of infantry would be made and that future vacancies in that post would be filled by lieutenant colonel commandants.

On January 1, 1781 a new regimental organization went into effect, having been adopted the previous November. Now the new organization of an infantry regiment was to be:

STAFF:	1 colonel, 1 lieutenant colonel, 1 major (or 1 lieutenant colonel commandant and 2 majors in lieu of the preceding), 1 adjutant, 1 quartermaster, 1 paymaster, 1 surgeon, 1 surgeon's mate, 1 sergeant major, 1 quartermaster sergeant, 1 drum major, 1 fife major
RECRUITING PARTY:	1 lieutenant, 1 drummer, 1 fifer
8 LINE OR: BATTALION COMPANIES EACH	1 captain, 1 lieutenant, 1 ensign, 5 sergeants, 1 drummer, 1 fifer, 68 corporals and privates

1 light company organized like a line company

TOTAL:	717 officers and men

In actual fact, most regiments were considerably below strength. One rarely finds battalions or regiments over 600 strong and only occasionally over 400. The typical infantry battalion would more likely consist of about 250 officers and enlisted men.

The smoothbore, flintlock musket with socket bayonet was the standard infantry weapon. The well equipped soldier carried 27-40 cartridges for it. Some men had to do duty with rifles or fowling pieces, but their lack of a bayonet and the rifle's slowness in loading placed line infantry armed with these substitutes at a severe disadvantage. The musket and bayonet was the normal armament of the rank and file (corporals and privates). Sergeants were usually similarly armed although many may have carried short sabers as well and some in the first campaigns might have had halberds in lieu of muskets. Drummers and fifers (who incidentally were more often adults than adolescents) sometimes had short sabers also. Officers were almost always armed with a sword or a dagger of some type and, in addition—when on foot—often with a spontoon or occasionally with a light musket or pistols. The field grade officers and the adjutant were usually mounted.

The drill (and consequently battle manuevers) were not standardized during the early part of the war, various British-authored systems of drill being used, but after the spring of 1778 Von Steuben's Regulations gradually superceded all others. Whatever drill and weapons were used, the best Continental infantry traded volleys with the best of the British regiments and acquitted themselves better than many of the finest European troops.

American infantry regiments maintained many of the typical military customs of 18th Century Europe. A few regiments had small bands of music of about eight pieces played by the regiment's fifers or other passing musicians hired with money taken from the officers' salaries. Each battalion was invariably weakened by the persistent problem of men being detached as officers' servants,[119] or wagoners, or artificers. On the march, the trains of the units were encumbered by the soldiers' women who invariably accompanied each battalion.

Infantry brigades were normally formed by a small staff and two to six battalions, usually all from the same state. Sometimes artillery and a wagon train were attached to the brigade. The brigade staff consisted of a brigadier general; a brigade major (usually a lieutenant or captain in rank, however) or aide who after May, 1778 was also a sub-inspector; and after March 27, 1777, a chaplain (no chaplain being allowed a battalion after this).[120] After May 27, 1778 a brigade quartermaster was also authorized. In August, 1778 each brigadier general was allowed 2 horses and a servant.

Two or three brigades and a small staff were sometimes formed into a division. Often the brigades were from the same state. A division was commanded by a major general who usually had about two aides (captains or lieutenants) and after May, 1778 an inspector (usually a major). The division was the largest subdivision of an army.

Invalid Corps   June 20, 1777 Congress resolved to raise a corps of invalids of eight companies each of 1 captain, 2 lieutenants, 2 ensigns, 5 sergeants, 6 corporals, 2 drummers, 2 fifers, and 100 men. These men were to serve in garrisons, magazines, and hospitals. The Invalid Corps was in keeping with British and European practice of the time and although many invalids were so damaged as to make them virtually useless, the practice remained general for many years afterwards. It is not stated whether, as in the British service, blind men were assigned to guard duty, but men missing a limb definitely were taken into the American corps. One other job the Continental Invalid Corps was to undertake was that of a military school for young gentlemen, therefore the noncommissioned officers were required to study mathematics.[121] This early attempt at a military academy apparently never got off the paper it was written on, but otherwise the corps performed the intended duties. On May 1, 1783 Congress ordered the Corps of Invalids disbanded and by June 18 of that year this had been done, leaving these maimed veterans to fend for themselves.[122]

COMMANDER: Colonel Lewis Nicola June 20, 1777-June, 1783.

Captain Matthew Irwin's Independent Company   A Pennsylvania independent company in the Continental service. It was taken into Malcolm's Additional Continental Regiment on May 12, 1777.

J

Colonel Henry Jackson's Additional Continental Regiment   Among the more successful of the additional regiments. Jackson's commission to raise the regiment was issued January 12, 1777. The regiment recruited mainly in the Boston area. On April 22, 1779, Henley's and William R. Lee's Additional Regiments were ordered consolidated into Jackson's Regiment. On June 23, 1780 steps were taken to incorporate Jackson's Regiment into the Massachusetts Line and on July 18, 1780 Jackson's unit became the 16th Massachusetts Regiment.[123]

COMMANDER: Colonel Henry Jackson

Colonel Henry Jackson's Continental Regiment   After November 3, 1783 the remaining infantry recruits of the Continental Army (largely Massachusetts men) were formed into Jackson's Continental Regiment (not to be confused with Jackson's Additional Continental Regiment of 1777-1780). The regiment is sometimes referred to by historians as the 1st American Regiment (not to be confused with the 1st American Regiment of late 1784-1791). Jackson's men were the last infantry to serve in the Continental Army. The regiment was disbanded by Congress on June 2, 1784.

K

Captain Samuel Kearsley's Independent Company   Accepted into Malcolm's Additional Continental Regiment on February 28, 1777.

Captain John Kingsbury's Independent North Carolina Artillery Company   On July 19, 1777 Kingsbury's Company was taken into the Continental service. The company had been raised previously. Sometime during 1778 or 1779 the company joined the Main Army. In November, 1779 the company was sent south with the rest of the North Carolina Continental Brigade[124] and together with the rest of the brigade was surrendered at Charleston on May 12, 1780. At that time the company numbered 64 men.[125]

Knowlton's Connecticut Rangers   A reconnaissance unit of 130 or 140 picked men from the Connecticut regiments as well as from other states. Washington activated the unit on August 26, 1776 on a temporary basis. The force served until it was captured at Fort Washington on November 16, 1776.[126]

COMMANDERS: Lieutenant Colonel Thomas Knowlton August 26, 1776-September 16, 1776.
Captain Stephen Brown September 16, 1776-October 1, 1776.

Major Andrew Colburn October 1, 1776-October 15, 1776.
Captain Lemuel Holmes October 15, 1776-November 16, 1776.

Colonel Knox's Artillery Regiment   Built up over the winter of 1775-76 using the remnants of Gridley's Regiment and all the artillerists then in Washington's army. As authorized on November 30, 1775 the regiment was to consist of 1 colonel, 2 lieutenant colonels, 2 majors, 1 adjutant, 1 quartermaster, 1 surgeon, 1 surgeon's mate, 1 chaplain, and twelve companies each of 1 captain, 1 captain lieutenant, 1 1st lieutenant, 2 2nd lieutenants, 3 sergeants, 3 corporals, 1 drummer, 1 fifer, 6 gunners, 6 bombardiers, and 30 mattrosses. The regiment's enlistments ran out at the end of 1776 and most of the men went home, thus causing a temporary crisis in the organization of that arm in the Main Army.[127]

COMMANDER: Colonel Henry Knox Commission dated November 17, 1775. Promoted to brigadier general December 27, 1776.

L

Captain Lamb's New York Artillery Company   The New York Artillery Company was part of the force authorized by Congress to be raised in New York at Continental expense on May 25, 1775. The 100 man company was activated in June, 1775 and subsequently served in the Canadian campaign of 1775. It was virtually destroyed in the attack on Quebec at the end of the year. Captain Lamb, who lost an eye and was captured, was subsequently exchanged and served briefly as commandant of the Northern Army's artillery during 1776.

   COMMANDER: Captain John Lamb June 30, 1775-captured December 31, 1775.

Lancaster County Independent Company   On January 18, 1777 a Continental company of 1 captain, 2 lieutenants, 1 ensign, 4 sergeants, 4 corporals, 1 drummer, 1 fifer, and 76 privates was raised to guard prisoners held in Lancaster County, Pennsylvania.[128] November 7, 1777 the company was annexed to the 10th Pennsylvania Regiment.

Lancaster County Rifle Company   In the latter part of 1775 a volunteer company of riflemen was raised in Lancaster County, Pennsylvania. By year's end it had been incorporated into Thompson's Pennsylvania Rifle Regiment.[129] *(See* Pennsylvania Rifle Regiment)

LaFayette's Light Division   This division served with great distinction in the Yorktown campaign of 1781.

DIVISION HEADQUARTERS: Major General Marquis de La Fayette, commanding
Major William Barber of New Jersey, division inspector

1ST BRIGADE HQ: Brigadier General Peter Muhlenberg of Virginia, brigade commander
Captain John Hobby of 10th Massachusetts Regt., brigade major

1ST BATTALION: Colonel Joseph Vose of Massachusetts, 8 Mass. companies

2ND BATTALION: Lt. Col. Gimat, 5 Conn. companies, 2 Mass. companies, 1 R.I. company

3RD BATTALION: Lt. Col. Francis Barber of New Jersey; 5 companies from N.J., N.H., etc.

2ND BRIGADE HQ: Brevet Brigadier General Moses Hazen of Canada, brigade commander
Captain Leonard Bleeker of 1st New York Regiment, brigade major

1ST BATTALION: Lt. Col. Ebenezer Huntington of Connecticut; 4 companies from Mass. and Conn.

2ND BATTALION: Lt. Col. Alexander Hamilton of New York; 2 N.Y. companies, 2 Conn. companies

3RD BATTALION: Lt. Col. John Laurens of South Carolina; 4 N.H. Conn., & Mass. companies

4TH BATTALION: Hazen's Canadian Regiment under Lt. Col. Antil

The division totaled about 1,500 men.

Captain Lee's Independent Artillery Company   On July 5, 1776 Congress authorized an independent artillery company to garrison Savannah, Georgia.[130] The 50 man company was raised. On February 19, 1778, Lee's Company merged with that of Captain Young.[131]

Lee's Legion   Also called Lee's Partisan Corps. On April 7, 1778 Captain Henry Lee of the 1st Regiment of Light Dragoons was promoted to major and authorized to increase his troop to two troops which were to form an independent corps. On May 28 of that year a third troop was authorized as well as a quartermaster for the corps who was to be ranked as a cornet. In November, 1778 Lee's Corps is noted as having 1 major, 1 quartermaster, 1 paymaster, 1 surgeon, 1 sergeant major, and three troops each apparently intended to have in addition to the troop commander, 1 lieutenant, 1 cornet, 2 sergeants, 4 corporals, 1 trumpeter, 1 farrier, and 30 troopers. One troop may have been dismounted and thus had no farrier and more privates.

On June 30, 1779 it was proposed that Captain McLane's Delaware company be incorporated with Lee's dismounted dragoons to form a fourth troop. On July 13, 1779 Congress approved this measure. McLane was a daring leader and his foot soldiers worked well with the light dragoons. In August the corps had around 200 officers and men in four troops, three mounted and one on foot. In addition to men from Virginia and Delaware, there were also numerous men from New Jersey, Maryland, and Connecticut in the unit. On February 14, 1780 Lee's men were to be reorganized into three troops and by General Orders of November 1, 1780 and effective January 1, 1781, the corps was to have three foot and three mounted troops.[132] Cavalry rank was ascribed to both mounted and dismounted members of the unit.

One source states Lee's Legion had a band. The Legion served with great distinction in the southern campaign of 1781. In 1782 Lee left his command and on June 13, 1782 General Greene split the Legion apart by assigning the cavalry to the mixed formation that included the 3rd and 4th Light Dragoons and the foot soldiers to Colonel Lauren's Light Infantry formation. Lee's officers were enraged by this and all of them resigned in protest, but the general coaxed them back and eventually the remnants were sent north and furloughed, probably sometime before mid-1783.[133]

COMMANDER: Major Henry Lee April 7, 1778-1782. Promoted to lieutenant colonel November 6, 1780.

Captain Lee's Maryland Artillery Company   Raised by Congressional resolve of November 22, 1777. Incorporated into the 4th Battalion of Continental Artillery by order of January 8, 1778.[134]

Colonel William R. Lee's Additional Continental Regiment   Lee got his commission to raise a regiment on January 1, 1777. He apparently did his recruiting in Massachusetts. His regiment consolidated with Jackson's Additional Regiment (which see) on April 22, 1779.

COMMANDERS: Colonel William Raymond Lee January 1, 1777-January 24, 1778.

Lieutenant Colonel William S. Smith January 24, 1778-April 29, 1779.

Corps of Light Infantry   Light infantry were supposed to be rapid moving scouts and skirmishers. They were intended to provide security for a close ordered force and to harass the main force of the enemy. Unlike line infantry they were trained to fight in the modern manner, firing at will and taking advantage of cover rather than firing in massed volleys and standing in ranks. Light infantry were accordingly supposed to be hardier, more agile, better marksmen, and generally more intelligent than the average infantryman.

The first Continental light infantry of any importance (excluding early rifle units) was Dearborn's temporary battalion formed in the summer of 1777 for service with the Northern Army and another temporary unit was formed shortly thereafter in the Main Army. These units were highly successful and after May 27, 1778 a company of light infantry was created in each infantry regiment. It was intended that during a campaign the light companies would be detached from their regiments and pooled into a corps of light infantry and that after each campaign the companies would be returned to their regiments to receive new recruits and equipment. This was accordingly the practice in the Main Army for the rest of the war.

The Corps of Light Infantry won renown at Stony Point and during the Yorktown campaign where it formed a division under LaFayette. The corps was certainly the best trained, equipped, and recruited part of the army. Some regiments apparently supplied two companies to it. The light infantry was armed with the musket, the bayonet with which it excelled, and perhaps the tomahawk. It is possible some of the officers carried light muskets as well as swords, but at Stony Point and Yorktown at least, the officers went into battle with spontoons rather than firearms. (*See* Dearborn's Light Infantry Battalion, General Gist's Light Corps, LaFayette's Light Division, Maryland-Delaware Light Infantry Battalion, Wayne's Light Infantry)

M

Machias Independent Artillery Company   On February 15, 1781 Congress voted to take over the pay, clothing, and subsistence of a 65 man artillery company which was to serve as a garrison for the port of Machias, Massachusetts. The men were to be enlisted for the usual period of three years or for the war.[135] Some of these men may have been former state troops. It is unconfirmed that this company was raised.

Main Army   The Main Army in the service of the thirteen states was that force gathered about the commander-in-chief, General George Washington. It was disbanded November 5, 1783 except for a small observation force under Major General Henry Knox which remained until the following June.

Colonel Malcolm's Additional Continental Regiment   This regiment was not created until April 30, 1777 and recruited in New York. For a time the independent companies of Catherwood, Doyle, Steel, and Wilkie were attached to the regiment, but they transferred to the 11th Pennsylvania on January 13, 1779. On April 22, 1779 This regiment was ordered merged with Spencer's Additional Continental Regiment (which see).

COMMANDER: Colonel William Malcolm

Marchesie Corps

Marchesie Corps Marchesie was a corruption of the French word for field or rural police. *See* Von Heer's Provost Troop of Light Dragoons.

Maryland Corps From about 1779 to 1781 three companies of Marylanders were garrisoned at Fort Pitt. The companies included men from the 1st through 8th Maryland Regiments and Rawlings' defunct corps.

Maryland Legion *See* Pulaski's Legion.

1st Maryland Regiment of 1777 The 1st Maryland Regiment was reorganized over the winter of 1776-77 using the remnants of Smallwood's Maryland Regiment as a cadre.[136] The regiment was demolished at the Battle of Camden on August 16, 1780 and its remnants were pooled into the Maryland Regiment (which see).[137]

COMMANDERS: Colonel Francis Ware December 10, 1776-February 18, 1777.
Colonel John H. Stone February 18, 1777-August 1, 1779.
Lieutenant Colonel Peter Adams August 1, 1779-January 1, 1781.

1st Maryland Regiment of 1781 With the arrival of large numbers of new recruits in the early months of 1781, the veteran Marylanders of the 1780 campaign were formed into the 1st Maryland Battalion (later formalized as the 1st Maryland Regiment).[138] The regiment returned only five companies on strength on January 1, 1782 and on January 1, 1783 one of the junior Maryland regiments (3rd or 4th) was incorporated into it bringing it up to the regulation nine companies.[139] After April 12, 1783 most of the veterans of the regiment were furloughed and the new enlistees were formed into the Maryland Battalion (which see).

COMMANDER: Colonel Otto Williams January 1, 1781-May 9, 1782
Lieutenant Colonel John Stewart May 9, 1782-December, 1782.
Lieutenant Colonel Levin Winder January 1, 1783-April 12, 1783.

2nd Maryland Regiment of 1777   The 2nd Maryland Regiment was created on December 10, 1776, utilizing the remnants of seven Maryland State Independent Companies as a cadre.[140] The regiment was decimated at Camden on August 16, 1780 and its remnants were pooled into the Maryland Regiment (which see).

COMMANDER: Colonel Thomas Price December 10, 1776-April 21, 1780. During the 1780 campaign, Lieutenant Colonel John Howard was generally in command.

2nd Maryland Regiment of 1781   This regiment was the 2nd Maryland Battalion of early 1781. It was formed from some of the first Marylanders to join the Southern Army after the disastrous campaign of 1780. It was soon formally known as the 2nd Maryland Regiment. The returns of January 1, 1782 credit the regiment with only five companies and on January 1, 1783 one of the junior Maryland Regiments (3rd or 4th) was incorporated into it bringing it up to the regulation nine companies. After April 12, 1783 most of the veterans of this regiment were furloughed and the new enlistees were formed into the Maryland Battalion (which see).

COMMANDER: Colonel John Gunby January 1, 1781-April 12, 1783.

3rd Maryland Regiment of 1777   Created December 10, 1776 as part of the Maryland quota. The regiment served until August 16, 1780 when it was decimated at Camden and its remnants were pooled into the Maryland Regiment.

COMMANDERS: Colonel Mordecai Gist December 10, 1776-January 9, 1779.
Lieutenant Colonel Nathaniel Ramsay January 10, 1779-January 1, 1781.

3rd Maryland Regiment of 1781   Late in 1780 Maryland took steps to raise two battalions for the stricken Southern Army.[141] This was done and by the next summer the 3rd and 4th Maryland Regiments were in the field. On January 1, 1782 they boasted only four companies apiece. On January 1, 1783 they were incorporated into the two senior regiments of the Maryland Line.

COMMANDER: Lieutenant Colonel Peter Adams January 1, 1781-January 1, 1783.

4th Maryland Regiment of 1777   This regiment had an organizational

65

history almost identical to the 3rd Maryland Regiment of 1777 (which see).

COMMANDER: Colonel Josias Hall December 10, 1776-January 1, 1781.

4th Maryland Regiment of 1781 This regiment had an organizational history identical to that of the 3rd Maryland Regiment of 1781 (which see).

COMMANDER: Lieutenant Colonel Thomas Woolford January 1, 1781-January 1, 1783.

5th Maryland Regiment of 1777 This regiment had an organizational history almost identical to the 3rd Maryland Regiment of 1777 (which see).

COMMANDERS: Colonel William Richardson December 10, 1776-October 22, 1779.
Lieutenant Colonel Thomas Woolford October 22, 1779-January 1, 1781.

5th Maryland Regiment of 1781 The officers of this regiment are found on a list dated June 1, 1781, but the author has found no evidence that the regiment was raised.

COMMANDER: Lieutenant Colonel Benjamin Ford

6th Maryland Regiment This regiment had an organizational history almost identical to that of the 3rd Maryland Regiment of 1777 (which see).

COMMANDER: Colonel Otto Williams December 10, 1776-January 1, 1781. During the 1780 campaign Lieutenant Colonel Benjamin Ford was usually in command as Williams was on staff duty.

7th Maryland Regiment This regiment had an organizational history almost identical to the 3rd Maryland Regiment of 1777 (which see).

COMMANDER: Colonel John Gunby Commissioned as colonel April 17, 1777-January 1, 1781.

8th Maryland Regiment *See* the German Battalion.

Maryland Additional Regiment or Battalion On July 27, 1780

Maryland sent General Washington notice they were raising another Continental battalion and in September the new recruits were sent to join the Southern Army.[142] These men joined the Maryland Regiment in November, 1780 and in early 1781 they were formed into the 2nd Maryland Battalion *(see* 2nd Maryland Regiment).

Maryland Regiment   After the defeat at Camden in August, 1781 Brigadier General Smallwood of Maryland and some of his dedicated subordinates gathered enough of their soldiers together for General Gates to form them into an effective regiment in September or October, 1780. Men were soon drafted out of this unit for a light battalion *(see* Maryland-Delaware Light Infantry Battalion), but new recruits soon appeared to refill the ranks *(see* Maryland Additional Regiment).[143] This regiment was later split into two battalions in 1781 *(see* 1st and 2nd Maryland Regiments of 1781).

Maryland-Delaware Light Infantry Battalion   On October 30, 1780 four companies were drafted out of the Maryland and Delaware Continentals in Gates' army and formed into a light infantry battalion which served well at Cowpens, although employed as conventional line infantry.[144] The battalion was broken up in the late winter of 1781 and the Delaware men separated to themselves while the Marylanders were placed in the 1st Maryland Regiment.
COMMANDER: Lieutenant Colonel John Howard

Maryland Battalion   After April 12, 1783 the Maryland Line recruits that remained were formed into a battalion. Most of them were apparently furloughed sometime between June 11, 1783 and September of that year and discharged November 15, 1783.
COMMANDER: Colonel John Gunby April 12, 1783-November 15, 1783.

Maryland Rifle Companies   On June 14, 1775 Congress called on Maryland to raise two rifle companies to serve Congress till the end of the year. Each company was to have 1 captain, 3 lieutenants, 4 sergeants, 4 corporals, 1 drummer or trumpeter, and 68 privates. The companies joined the Continental Army at Boston. Some of the riflemen were apparently detached for service in Canada and many of the rest went home when their enlistments expired at the end of the year. Those men that stayed with the army were apparently absorbed into Stephenson's Maryland and Virginia Rifle Regiment (which see) in mid-1776. One of the companies was under Captain Michael Cresap, but on October 21, 1775 he was replaced by Moses Rawlings. The other company was commanded by Captain Thomas Price.

Maryland and Virginia Rifle Regiment   *See* Stephenson's Maryland and Virginia Rifle Regiment.

Colonel David Brewer's Massachusetts Battalion   This battalion was taken into the Continental Army around Boston in June of 1775 and served till December of that year.
>   COMMANDERS: Colonel David Brewer June 17, 1775-October 24, 1775.
>   Lieutenant Colonel Rufus Putnam October 24, 1775-December, 1775.

Colonel Jonathan Brewer's Massachusetts Battalion   This was one of twelve Massachusetts battalions created by the Massachusetts legislature on May 19, 1775. A battalion was to consist of ten companies, each company having 1 captain or field grade officer, 1 lieutenant, 1 ensign, 4 sergeants, 1 drummer, 1 fifer, and 50 privates. The field grade officers of the battalion did double duty as company commanders. It had originally been planned to have 100 man companies, but the reluctance of men to serve under officers they did not know prevented this.[145] The battalions were taken into the Continental Army on June 14, 1775 and served until that December.

Colonel Bridge's Massachusetts Battalion   This battalion was formed May 27, 1775 and served until December of that year.
>   COMMANDER: Colonel Ebenezer Bridge

Colonel Cotton's Massachusetts Battalion   Colonel Cotton's Battalion was one of six created by the Massachusetts legislature on May 27, 1775 and taken into the Continental Army on June 14, 1775. It served until December of that year.
>   COMMANDER: Colonel Theophilus Cotton

Colonel Danielson's Massachusetts Battalion   This battalion had an organizational history almost identical to Cotton's Massachusetts Battalion (which see).
>   COMMANDER: Colonel Timothy Danielson

Colonel Doolittle's Massachusetts Battalion   This battalion had an organizational history almost identical to Cotton's Massachusetts Battalion (which see).

COMMANDERS: Colonel Ephraim Doolittle May 27, 1775-October, 1775.

Lieutenant Colonel Benjamin Holden October, 1775-December, 1775.

Colonel Fellow's Massachusetts Battalion   This battalion was created May 31, 1775 by the Massachusetts government and was taken into the Continental Army June 14, 1775. It served until December of that year.

COMMANDER: Colonel John Fellows

Colonel Frye's Massachusetts Battalion   This battalion had an organizational history almost identical to Jonathan Brewer's Massachusetts Battalion (which see).

COMMANDER: Colonel James Frye

Colonel Gardner's Massachusetts Battalion   Gardner's Battalion was created June 2, 1775 and taken into the Continental Army June 14, 1775. It served until December of that year.

COMMANDERS: Colonel Thomas Gardner June 2, 1775-July 3, 1775.

Colonel William Bond July 3, 1775-December, 1775.

Colonel Gerrish's Massachusetts Battalion   This battalion had an organizational history almost identical to Jonathan Brewer's Massachusetts Battalion (which see).

COMMANDERS: Colonel Samuel Gerrish May 19, 1775-August 19, 1775

Lieutenant Colonel Loammi Baldwin August 19, 1775-December, 1775.

Colonel Glover's Massachusetts Battalion   This battalion had an organizational history almost identical to Jonathan Brewer's Massachusetts Battalion (which see).

COMMANDER: Colonel John Glover

Colonel Heath's Massachusetts Battalion   This battalion had an organizational history almost identical to Jonathan Brewer's Massachusetts Battalion (which see).

COMMANDERS: Colonel William Heath May 19, 1775-June 22, 1775.
Colonel John Greaton July 1, 1775-December, 1775.

Colonel Learned's Massachusetts Battalion   This battalion had an organizational history almost identical to Jonathan Brewer's Massachusetts Battalion (which see).

COMMANDER: Colonel Ebenezer Learned

Colonel Little's Massachusetts Battalion   This battalion had an organizational history almost identical to Jonathan Brewer's Massachusetts Battalion (which see).

COMMANDER: Colonel Moses Little

Colonel Mansfield's Massachusetts Battalion   This battalion had an organizational history almost identical to Cotton's Massachusetts Battalion (which see).

COMMANDERS: Colonel John Mansfield May 27, 1775-September 15, 1775.
Lieutenant Colonel Israel Hutchison September 15, 1775-December, 1775.

Colonel John Nixon's Massachusetts Battalion   This battalion had an organizational history almost identical to Jonathan Brewer's Massachusetts Battalion (which see).

COMMANDER: Colonel John Nixon

Colonel Paterson's Massachusetts Battalion   This battalion had an organizational history almost identical to Cotton's Massachusetts Battalion (which see).

COMMANDER: Colonel John Paterson

Colonel Phinney's Massachusetts Battalion   This battalion had an organizational history almost identical to Jonathan Brewer's Massachusetts Battalion (which see).

COMMANDER: Colonel Edmund Phinney

Colonel Prescott's Massachusetts Battalion   This battalion had an organizational history almost identical to Jonathan Brewer's Massachusetts Battalion (which see).

COMMANDER: Colonel William Prescott

Colonel Reed's Massachusetts Battalion Reed's Battalion was created May 18, 1775 by the Massachusetts government and taken into the Continental Army on June 14, 1775. It served until December of that year.

COMMANDER: Colonel Joseph Reed

Colonel Sargent's Massachusetts Battalion This battalion had an organizational history almost identical to Jonathan Brewer's Massachusetts Battalion (which see).

COMMANDER: Colonel Paul Sargent

Colonel Scammon's Massachusetts Battalion Scammon's battalion was created in May, 1775 and taken into the Continental Army on June 14. It served until December of that year.

COMMANDER: Colonel James Scammon

Colonel Thomas' Massachusetts Battalion This battalion had an organizational history almost identical to Jonathan Brewer's Massachusetts Battalion (which see).

COMMANDERS: Colonel John Thomas May 19, 1775-June 30, 1775.
Colonel John Bailey July 1, 1775-December, 1775.

Colonel Walker's Massachusetts Battalion This battalion was created May 23, 1775 and was taken into the Continental Army on June 14. It served until December of 1775.

COMMANDER: Colonel Timothy Walker

Colonel Ward's Massachusetts Battalion Ward's battalion was created on May 23, 1775 and taken into the Continental Army on June 14. It served until December, 1775.

COMMANDERS: Colonel Artemus Ward May 23, 1775-June 17, 1775.
Colonel Jonathan Ward June 17, 1775-December, 1775.

Colonel Whitcomb's Massachusetts Battalion   This battalion was created on June 3, 1775 and taken into the Continental Army on June 14. It served until that December.

COMMANDER: Colonel Asa Whitcomb

Colonel Woodbridge's Massachusetts Battalion   This battalion was created on June 16, 1775 and taken into the Continental Army where it served until that December.

COMMANDER: Colonel Benjamin Woodbridge

Massachusetts Independent Infantry Companies   Sometime in late July or August, 1775, four independent companies of Massachusetts infantrymen were taken into Continental pay. General Washington, however, was uncertain whether they were a part of his army or not. These companies existed until at least June, 1776.[146]

1st Massachusetts Regiment   Colonel Vose's commission to raise a regiment of the Massachusetts quota was granted January 1, 1777 and the regiment was subsequently numbered the 1st Massachusetts. The regiment served until discharged on November 3, 1783. A few of its recruits then went into Jackson's Continental Regiment.

COMMANDER: Colonel Joseph Vose January 1, 1777-November 3, 1783.

2nd Massachusetts Regiment   John Bailey's regiment, subsequently numbered the 2nd Massachusetts, was created November 1, 1776 and served until November 3, 1783 when it was discharged. A few of its recruits then went into Jackson's Continental Regiment.

COMMANDERS: Colonel John Bailey November 1, 1776-October 21, 1780.
Lieutenant Colonel Ezra Badlam October 21, 1780-January 1, 1781.
Lieutenant Colonel Ebenezer Sprout January 1, 1781-November 3, 1783.

3rd Massachusetts Regiment   The regiment subsequently numbered the 3rd Massachusetts was created on November 1, 1776. The 3rd Massachusetts Regiment served until November 3, 1783 when most of the recruits of which it was then composed were discharged and the rest placed in Jackson's Continental Regiment.

COMMANDERS: Colonel John Greaton November 1, 1776-January 7, 1783.
Lieutenant Colonel James Mellen January 7, 1783-June 12, 1783.
Colonel Michael Jackson June 12, 1783-November 3, 1783.

4th Massachusetts Regiment   The regiment subsequently numbered the 4th Massachusetts was created on January 1, 1777. The regiment served until November 3, 1783 when most of the recruits of which it was then composed were discharged and the rest placed in Jackson's Continental Regiment.

COMMANDERS: Colonel William Shepard January 1, 1777-January 1, 1783.
Colonel Henry Jackson January 1, 1783-November 3, 1783.

5th Massachusetts Regiment   This regiment was created on November 1, 1776 and served until it was disbanded on June 12, 1783.

COMMANDERS: Colonel Rufus Putnam November 1, 1776-January 7, 1783.
Lieutenant Colonel David Cobb January 7, 1783-June 12, 1783.

6th Massachusetts Regiment   This regiment was created on November 1, 1776 and served until it was disbanded on June 12, 1783.

COMMANDERS: Colonel Thomas Nixon November 1, 1776-January 1, 1781.
Lieutenant Colonel Calvin Smith January 1, 1781-January 1, 1783.
Colonel Benjamin Tupper January 1, 1783-June 12, 1783.

7th Massachusetts Regiment   This regiment was created on November 1, 1776 and served until it was disbanded on June 12, 1783.

COMMANDER: Colonel Ichabod Alden November 1, 1776-November 10, 1778.
Lieutenant Colonel John Brooks November 11, 1778-June 12, 1783.

8th Massachusetts Regiment   This regiment was created on November 1, 1776 and served until it was disbanded on June 12, 1783.

COMMANDER: Colonel Michael Jackson November 1, 1776-June 12, 1783.

9th Massachusetts Regiment   This regiment was created November 1, 1776 and served until January 1, 1783 when in compliance with orders of December 24, 1782 it was disbanded.[147]

COMMANDERS: Colonel James Wesson November 1, 1776-January 1, 1781.
Colonel Henry Jackson January 1, 1781-January 1, 1783.

10th Massachusetts Regiment   This regiment was created November 6, 1776 and served until January 1, 1783 when in compliance with orders of December 24, 1782 it was disbanded.

COMMANDERS: Colonel Thomas Marshall November 6, 1776-January 1, 1781.
Colonel Benjamin Tupper January 1, 1781-January 1, 1783.

11th Massachusetts Regiment   This regiment was created on November 6, 1776 and served until officially broken up on January 1, 1781.

COMMANDERS: Colonel Ebenezer Francis November 6, 1776-July 7, 1777.
Colonel Benjamin Tupper July 7, 1777-January 1, 1781.

12th Massachusetts Regiment   This regiment was created on November 6, 1776 and served until broken up officially on January 1, 1781.

COMMANDERS: Colonel Samuel Brewer November 6, 1776-September 29, 1778.
Lieutenant Colonel Ebenezer Sprout September 29, 1778-January 1, 1781.

13th Massachusetts Regiment   This regiment was created January 1, 1777 and served until officially broken up on January 1, 1781.

COMMANDERS: Colonel Edmund Wigglesworth January 1, 1777-March 10, 1779.
Lieutenant Colonel Calvin Smith March 10, 1779-January 1, 1781.

14th Massachusetts Regiment   This regiment was created January 1, 1777 and served until officially broken up on January1, 1781.
COMMANDER: Colonel Gamaliel Bradford January 1, 1777-January 1, 1781.

15th Massachusetts Regiment   This regiment was created on January 1, 1777 and served until officially broken up on January 1, 1781.
COMMANDER: Colonel Timothy Bigelow January 1, 1777-January 1, 1781.

16th Massachusetts Regiment   On July 18, 1780 Colonel Henry Jackson's Additional Continental Regiment became the 16th Massachusetts. The regiment was broken up on January 1, 1781.
COMMANDER: Colonel Henry Jackson July 23, 1780-January 1, 1781.

Lieutenant Colonel Hezekiah Mayham's Legion   In mid-1781 General Greene created a Continental legion in South Carolina under Colonel Mayham. The legion consisted of 80 men.[148]In February, 1782 the legion was surprised and scattered by the enemy. Some time after March 29, 1782 Horry's Regiment was merged in Mayham's and the whole transferred to the state service,[149] but Mayham's capture shortly thereafter spelled the end of the legion. (*See* Horry's South Carolina Regiment.)

Captain Allen McLane's Troop   Allen McLane began his military career as a lieutenant in the Delaware militia. In 1776 he joined Washington's army and by the end of the year he seems to have been leading a ragtag, but mounted troop which appears to have entered the Continental pay. The troop seems to have been taken into Colonel Patton's Additional Continental Regiment during 1777 and served in the regiment until around January 13, 1779 when it was transferred to the Delaware Regiment.[150] On July 13, 1779 the troop or company was transferred again, this time to Lee's Legion (which see).[151] The company served with the Legion until its break up upon which it was assigned to Lauren's Light

Infantry Corps until disbanded. McLane's original followers seem to have been mounted, but after 1777 it is almost certain they served exclusively as light infantry.

Middle Department   The Middle Department was created by Congress on February 27, 1776 as a military administrative district comprising New York, New Jersey, Pennsylvania, modern Delaware, and Maryland. A major general, two brigadier generals, and a staff were allowed for the department.[152] This department apparently faded out after 1776.

Militia   Almost all able bodied males in the thirteen colonies were required by law to be enrolled in the militia of their colony. Each militiaman was required to have either a musket or a rifle, ammunition, and either a bayonet, sword, or tomahawk. Some colonies specified other items as well and militia officers and cavalry were of course required to have appropriate equipment.

American militia were supposed to serve without pay, for short periods of time only, and only within their own state. They were to have inspection and drill periodically. The militia were generally organized into county or multicounty regiments and parish or town companies in the English tradition. In urban areas elite volunteer militia units existed in 1775, notably the Massachusetts Cadets, the Honorable Artillery Company of Boston, the Connecticut Governor's Foot Guard, the Rhode Island Train of Artillery, New York dragoon, infantry, and artillery units, and several corps in Philadelphia. These volunteer companies, although most never saw active service, furnished basic training to several notable Continental officers.

Generally, however, the American militia system varied from theory. Drill and inspection, except possibly in Virginia, were seldom held. The militiamen rarely mobilized in accord with their old county regiment system. Usually they were paid (at least in theory) by either Congress or their state for service and sometimes they were called out for long term service and service in other states.

The American militia was fairly effective, however. From out of the mass of common militia, minuteman or alarm companies who had their full equipment and were ready to use it on short notice were formed. Other militia men volunteered to fight and formed volunteer tactical organizations for field service when danger threatened or sometimes when the bounty was high for doing so. Some militia performed valiantly in the field and the riflemen from the frontiers of Virginia and the Carolinas were fierce opponents to the British, once driven to espouse the rebel cause.

On the whole, American militia were well armed. Almost everyone reporting for field service had a gun of some sort and this made the militia potent if well led and commanded. The Continental Army was a major factor in the winning of independence, but so were the numbers of militia which the rebel states' governments controlled.

Minutemen   *See* Militia.

Morgan's Rifle Corps   During the summer of 1777 General Washington selected 500 riflemen from the Main Army and formed them into a corps under Colonel Daniel Morgan. Most of the men in the corps were woodsmen and good hunters and so were adjudged a fit body to counter enemy light troops and Indian allies. The corps was sent to join the Northern Army and in September, 1777 served with great distinction in the American victory at Saratoga. After the victory, the corps rejoined the Main Army in the winter of 1777-78 and was broken up, as it was strictly a creature of emergency. This corps should not be confused with the Virginia rifle company commanded by Morgan in 1775.

Captain Morris' Independent Artillery Company   On July 5, 1776 Congress authorized an artillery company to garrison Sunbury, Georgia. This 50-man company was accordingly raised.[153] No further information.

N

Captain John Nelson's Independent Rifle Company   Captain Nelson's Company was taken into the Continental service on January 30, 1776. Intended for service in Canada, there is no evidence that it ever joined the Northern Army. This company of Pennsylvanians had a strength of 1 captain, 3 lieutenants, 4 sergeants, 4 corporals, and 70 privates.[154] On November 15, 1776 Nelson was made a captain in the 9th Pennsylvania Regiment and it is highly unlikely that his rifle company survived that date as an independent formation.

Thomas Nelson's Cavalry Troop   The troop seems to have been raised in the spring of 1778 and was disbanded at Philadelphia around August 1, 1778. General Thomas Nelson, the commander of the Virginia militia, had raised the troop at his own expense, but Congress had no use for it. General Washington wrote a letter of sympathy to his old friend shortly thereafter stating his wish that they could have campaigned together.[155] Nelson later, in 1781 in the dual role of state governor and militia commander of Virginia, took part in the Yorktown campaign.

New Hampshire Rangers   Created on the initiative of the New Hampshire government, in the summer of 1775 these three companies, each nominally of 66 officers and men, were brigaded under Colonel Timothy Bedel, a veteran of the French and Indian War.

The rangers were offered to Washington's army, but he refused them, saying he had no need for rangers and that the unit should be offered to General Schuyler's Separate Army. This was done and Schuyler accepted them. The rangers served in Canada until their enlistments ran out at the end of 1775. On January 20, 1776 steps were taken to reraise the rangers on the same organizational plan as the battalions in the Main Army.[156] Congress refused to accept the upkeep of Bedel's Rangers, however, owing to organizational defects[157] and in July, 1776 Bedel was ordered court-martialed for cowardice.[158] Despite the low regard of him held by Congress, Bedel remained popular in his home state. In April, 1778 Bedel was accordingly assigned by General Gates, commander of the Northern Department, to reraise his regiment.[159] This regiment had a very touch and go existence as Congress was none too willing to maintain it. Finally the corps, now under Major Whitcomb, was ordered disbanded by January 1, 1781. This was not done, however, as a letter from General Washington dated March 12, 1781 scolds Whitcomb for having not yet disbanded his men.[160]

1st New Hampshire Regiment of 1775   This regiment was created April 23, 1775 and by June had a strength of ten companies each supposedly of 62 men. The regiment was taken into the Continental Army around Boston by Congressional resolve of June 14, 1775 and served to the end of the year.

> COMMANDER: Colonel John Stark April 23, 1775-December, 1775.

1st New Hampshire Regiment of 1777   This regiment was created after November 8, 1776 during the reorganization of the Continental Army for long term service. The regiment served until March 1, 1782 when the New Hampshire Line was reorganized.

> COMMANDERS: Colonel John Stark November 8, 1776-March 23, 1777
> Colonel Joseph Cilley April 2, 1777-January 1, 1781
> Colonel Alexander Scammell January 1, 1781-October 6, 1781
> Lieutenant Colonel Henry Dearborn October 6, 1781-March 1, 1782

2nd New Hampshire Regiment of 1775   This regiment was created May 20, 1775 and was in fact junior to the regiment that the state legislature designated 3rd after a lengthy dispute. The regiment entered the Continental service after the resolution of June 14, 1775 and served until the end of the year.

COMMANDER: Colonel Enoch Poor May 20, 1775-December, 1775

2nd New Hampshire Regiment of 1777   This regiment had an organizational history similar to the 1st New Hampshire of 1777 (which see).

COMMANDERS: Colonel Enoch Poor November 8, 1776-February 21, 1777

Lieutenant Colonel Nathan Hale February 21, 1777-September 23, 1780.   Hale was promoted to colonel on April 2, 1777. He was not the same man as Nathan Hale of Connecticut, the famous spy.

Lieutenant Colonel George Reid September 23, 1780-March 1, 1782

3rd New Hampshire Regiment of 1775   Created April 28, 1775, the regiment was designated 3rd after a prolonged dispute over seniority. The regiment had 1 colonel, 1 lieutenant colonel, 1 major, 1 adjutant, 1 quartermaster, and ten companies. Each company had 1 captain, 1 lieutenant, 1 ensign, 4 sergeants, 4 corporals, 1 drummer, 1 fifer, and 32 to 51 privates.[161] The regiment was taken into the Continental Army around Boston on June 14, 1775 and served until the end of the year.

COMMANDER: Colonel James Reed April 28, 1775-December, 1775.

3rd New Hampshire Regiment of 1777   This regiment was created after November 8, 1776 and served until January 1, 1781 when its remaining men were incorporated into the 1st New Hampshire.

COMMANDER: Colonel Alexander Scammell November 8, 1776-January 1, 1781.

New Hampshire Regiment   On March 1, 1782 the remaining New Hampshire Continentals were merged into one regiment which served until November 3-5, 1783 when most of the new enlistees of which the regiment was then composed were discharged and the rest joined Jackson's Continental Regiment (which see).

COMMANDER: Lieutenant Colonel George Reid March 1, 1782-November 3, 1783.

New Jersey Artillery Companies   On February 13, 1776 an East Artillery Company and a West Artillery Company were created to defend the state. Each company consisted of 1 captain, 1 captain lieutenant, 1 1st lieutenant, 1 2nd lieutenant, 1 fireworker, 4 sergeants, 4 corporals, 1 bombardier, and 50 mattrosses.[162] In December, 1776 these state companies were attached to the Continental Army and were subsequently absorbed into the 4th Battalion of Continental Artillery (which see).

New Jersey Light Horse Troop   Early in 1778 a troop was formed in New Jersey for Continental service, but General Washington, although he had high regard for the troop commander, refused to take the unit into his army.[163] So far as known, this troop was never taken into Continental service.

1st New Jersey Regiment of 1776   On October 9, 1775 the Continental Congress resolved that two battalions should be raised in New Jersey at Continental expense. Each battalion was to have eight companies each of 1 captain, 1 lieutenant, 1 ensign, 4 sergeants, 4 corporals, and 68 privates. Not until November 4, 1775, however, were field officers elected for the units. By the end of November recruiting was underway.[164] The 1st New Jersey served through the next year until its enlistments ran out at the year's end and a virtually new regiment with its old number had to be raised for the subsequent campaigns.

COMMANDERS: Colonel William Alexander, Lord Stirling November 7, 1775-March 1, 1776.
Colonel William Winds (formerly the lieutenant colonel) March 7, 1776-November 20, 1776.

1st New Jersey Regiment of 1777   This regiment was organized in late 1776 and early 1777 and served until about June 12, 1783 when its remaining men were furloughed, being ultimately discharged November 5, 1783.

COMMANDERS: Colonel Silas Newcomb November 28, 1776-January 1, 1777.
Colonel Matthias Ogden January 1, 1777-c. April 21, 1783.

2nd New Jersey Regiment of 1776   This unit had a history similar to the 1st New Jersey Regiment of 1776.

2nd New Jersey Regiment of 1777

COMMANDERS: Colonel William Maxwell November 8, 1775-October 23, 1776.

Lieutenant Colonel Israel Shreve October 23, 1776-November 20, 1776.

2nd New Jersey Regiment of 1777   This regiment was organized in late 1776 and early 1777 and served until about June 12, 1783 when it was furloughed. Its men were officially discharged on November 5, 1783. It should be noted that during the Yorktown campaign of 1781 the regiment was temporarily combined with the 1st New Jersey to form one large unit 600 strong. The 2nd New Jersey had a small band of music.

COMMANDERS: Colonel Israel Shreve November 28, 1776-January 1, 1781.

Colonel Elias Dayton January 1, 1781-January 7, 1783.

Colonel Francis Barber January 7, 1783-February 11, 1783.

Lieutenant Colonel Jonathan Forman February 11, 1783-c. April, 1783.

3rd New Jersey Regiment of 1776   On February 9, 1776 officers were elected by Congress for a third New Jersey Battalion.[165] By March recruiting had begun and the battalion served on to year's end when its enlistments ran out and a new 3rd New Jersey had to be raised for the next campaigns.

COMMANDER: Colonel Elias Dayton January 18, 1776-November, 1776.

3rd New Jersey Regiment of 1777   This regiment was organized in late 1776 and early 1777 and served until broken up by General Orders of November 1, 1780 effective January 1, 1781.

COMMANDER: Colonel Elias Dayton November, 1776-January 1, 1781.

4th New Jersey Regiment   This regiment was created in late November, 1776 to fill the state's quota of Continental battalions for the next campaign. So far as known, the colonel never joined his unit and presumably the regiment never was well organized. Around July 1, 1778 the regiment was broken up and its men taken into other regiments of the New Jersey Line.

COMMANDERS: Colonel Ephraim Martin Elected November, 1776. Never joined his unit.

Lieutenant Colonel David Brearley November 28, 1776-January 1, 1777.
Lieutenant Colonel David Rhea January 1, 1777-July 1, 1778.

5th New Jersey Regiment   *See* Spencer's Additional Continental Regiment.

New York Levies of Militia and State Troops   On April 2, 1781 New York voted to raise two regiments of militia to serve until December 1, 1781 and two regiments of state troops to serve three years. Congress voted to pay and supply these men during their term of service, yet at the same time not make them a part of the Continental Army.[166] As late as 1782-83 some of these troops remained under the command of Colonel Marinus Willett, still not a part of the Continental Army, but paid by Continental funds and cooperating with the Continental Army.

New York Rangers   During the 1778 campaign, a temporary ranger company and three provincial (state) ranger companies saw service. These men apparently considered themselves Continentals, but General Washington later ruled that owing to the incorrect manner of their mustering this was not so.[167] Quasi-Continental rangers from New York apparently served in the next year along the frontiers, however.

1st New York Regiment of 1775   On May 25, 1775 Congress approved a plan that called for New York to raise three thousand men at Continental expense to safeguard its territory.[168] By the end of June, officers had been appointed by the New York legislature for four infantry regiments and by the end of July the units were on their way to the Canadian frontier. Each regiment was to have 1 colonel, 1 lieutenant colonel, 1 major, 1 adjutant, 1 quartermaster, 1 surgeon, and ten companies. Each company was to have 1 captain, 2 lieutenants, 3 sergeants, 3 corporals, 1 drummer, 1 fifer, and 64 privates. The men were enlisted for only a few months, but in November most of them were persuaded to reenlist for six months. By the following April, however, most of the surviving men had had enough of the war. Some of these veterans reenlisted in Nicholson's New York Regiment, the rest returned home on the expiration of their enlistments.

COMMANDERS: Colonel Alexander McDougall June 30, 1775-November 3, 1775.

Lieutenant Colonel Rudolphus Ritzema November 3, 1775-March 28, 1776. Ritzema was promoted to colonel on November 28, 1775.

1st New York Regiment of 1776   On March 8, 1776 the Continental Congress elected field officers for four new battalions from New York.[169] Unlike the previous four of 1775 which were then in the process of dissolution, the new battalions were apparently intended to serve with the Main Army. The regiments were accordingly raised and served until the year's end when their enlistments expired, necessitating massive reorganization.

COMMANDER: Colonel Goose Van Shaik March 8, 1776-c. December, 1776.

1st New York Regiment of 1777   This last unit to be known as the 1st New York Regiment was organized between November, 1776 and early 1777. The regiment served through the war and was apparently furloughed about June 12, 1783 and discharged that November.

COMMANDER: Colonel Goose Van Shaik c. November, 1776-November 3, 1783.

2nd New York Regiment of 1775   This regiment had a history very similar to the 1st New York Regiment of 1775 (which see).

COMMANDER: Colonel Goose Van Shaik June 28, 1775-March 8, 1776.

2nd New York Regiment of 1776   This regiment had a history similar to the 1st New York Regiment of 1776 (which see).

COMMANDERS: Colonel James Clinton March 8, 1776-August 29, 1776.
Lieutenant Colonel Peter Gansevoort August 29, 1776-November 3, 1776.

2nd New York Regiment of 1777   This regiment had a history similar to the 1st New York Regiment of 1777 (which see).

COMMANDER: Colonel Philip Van Cortland November 21, 1776-November 3, 1783.

3rd New York Regiment of 1775   This regiment had a history similar to the 1st New York Regiment of 1775 (which see).

COMMANDER: Colonel James Clinton June 30, 1775-March,
1776.

3rd New York Regiment of 1776   This regiment had a history similar
to the 1st New York Regiment of 1776 (which see).
COMMANDER: Colonel Rudolphus Ritzema March 28, 1776-
November 21, 1776.

3rd New York Regiment of 1777   This 3rd New York Regiment was
organized between November, 1776 and early 1777. It was disbanded by General Orders effective January 1, 1781 and its
remaining enlisted men were incorporated into the two senior regiments of the New York Line.
COMMANDER: Colonel Peter Gansevoort November 21,
1776-January 1, 1781.

4th New York Regiment of 1775   This regiment had a history similar
to the 1st New York Regiment of 1775 (which see).
COMMANDER: Colonel James Holmes June 30, 1775-
December, 1775.

4th New York Regiment of 1776   This regiment had a history similar
to the 1st New York Regiment of 1776 (which see).
COMMANDER: Colonel Cornelius Wynkoop March 8, 1776-
November, 1776.

4th New York Regiment of 1777   This regiment had a history similar
to the 3rd New York Regiment of 1777 (which see).
COMMANDERS: Colonel Henry Beekman Livingston No-
vember 21, 1776-January 13, 1779.
Lieutenant Colonel Frederick Weisenfels
January 13, 1779-January 1, 1781.

5th New York Regiment   June 26, 1776 Colonel Lewis Dubois was
appointed by Congress to raise a Continental battalion.[170] This he
did using the remnants of his former unit, Nicholson's New York
Regiment, for a cadre. The regiment served in the Northern
Department. On November 21, 1776 the regiment was designated
the 5th Regiment of the New York Line. On October 6, 1777 most
of the regiment was captured at Fort Montgomery and the remnants gradually faded away.[171]
COMMANDERS: Colonel Lewis Dubois June 26, 1776-
December 22, 1779.

Colonel Marinus Willett December 22, 1779-January 1, 1781. Willett's command existed only on paper, however.

Nicholson's New York Regiment   Raised from remnants of the New York infantry of the 1775 Canadian campaign and new recruits, this unit was raised to comply with Congress' resolution of January 8, 1776.[172] Nicholson's Regiment was reorganized under Colonel Dubois in mid year. *See* 5th New York Regiment.

COMMANDER: Colonel John Nicholson March 8, 1776-June, 1776.

North Carolina Light Horse   The corps is referred to sometimes as rangers, sometimes as light horse. Independent troops of light horse had existed briefly in 1775, but Congress had refused them for Continental service.[173] In April, 1776 North Carolina once more raised three ranger troops for the Continental service. Each troop was to have 1 captain, 1 lieutenant, 1 cornet, and 30 privates. What became of the troops during the remainder of 1776 is somewhat of a mystery. Sometime between May and July of 1777, General Nash authorized a Corps of Light Dragoons, yet a letter from Washington that August states the Corps had a year and a half to serve and during 1777 Continentals were generally enlisted for three years or for the war.[174] The implication is that the ranger troops of 1776 were persuaded to extend their services for an additional period as the Corps of Light Dragoons. At any rate, in August, 1777 eighty troopers plus officers arrived at Philadelphia on their way to join the Main Army. When Washington received information about this small force, he recommended that its horses be sold at once as unfit for service and the men be drafted into Baylor's Regiment of Light Dragoons, their officers commanding them in rotation.[175] It is not certain how closely Washington's recommendations were followed. On September 10, 1777 Congress elected a paymaster for the North Carolina Light Horse,[176] implying the corps remained an independent formation. A subsequent letter from Cosimo de Medici, an officer of the North Carolina Light Horse, indicates he was working for Colonel Bland while trying to obtain a loan to mount his men.[177] De Medici seems to have been unsuccessful in his attempts to raise money. On January 1, 1779 it seems the North Carolina Light Horse were discharged.

North Carolina Rangers   *See* North Carolina Light Horse.

1st North Carolina Regiment of 1775   On June 26, 1775 Congress authorized one thousand men to be raised in North Carolina. In September the 1st and 2nd North Carolina Regiments were organized and served through the year. Each regiment was to consist of field officers, an adjutant, and ten companies each of 1 captain, 1 lieutenant, 1 ensign, and 50 men.[178]

COMMANDER: Colonel James Moore September 1, 1775-March, 1776.

1st North Carolina Regiment of 1776   In March, 1776 the 1st North Carolina Regiment was reorganized and on May 7, 1776 approved for the Continental service. Each North Carolina regiment at this time was to have 1 colonel, 1 lieutenant colonel, 1 major, 1 adjutant, 1 quartermaster, 1 surgeon, 1 commissary of stores, 1 wagon master, 1 sergeant major, 1 quartermaster sergeant, 1 drum major, and eight companies. Each company was to have 1 captain, 2 lieutenants, 1 ensign, 4 sergeants, 4 corporals, 2 drummers, 1 fifer, and 76 privates.[179] The regiment served in its home state through 1776, then was reorganized and sent north to join Washington. On May 29, 1778 this regiment along with the 2nd and 3rd North Carolina were brought up to strength with the men of the 4th, 5th, and 6th Regiments.[180] In late 1779 and early 1780 the men of this regiment along with those of the rest of the North Carolina regiments were formed into three regiments. *See* 1st North Carolina Regiment of 1780.

COMMANDERS: Colonel Francis Nash April 10, 1776-February 5, 1777.
Colonel Thomas Clark February 5, 1777-1780.

1st North Carolina Regiment of 1780   At the end of 1779 and the beginning of 1780 the North Carolina Line was reorganized into three regiments. All of them were captured at Charleston on May 12, 1780.

1st North Carolina Regiment of 1781   After the disaster at Charleston there were no North Carolina Continentals for a time. In October, 1780 Congress set the quota for North Carolina at four battalions, but the presence of the enemy prevented recruiting. Finally an American "victory" came at Guilford Courthouse in February, 1781. North Carolina militiamen fought at Guilford Courthouse. Faced by some of the best soldiers in the world, a number of these militiamen broke and ran. Although the circumstances of their flight are debatable in the eyes of history, five hundred of these militiamen were sentenced to the Continental service for one year by the state's Council Extraordinary for alledged cowardice.[181] With this act, the North Carolina Line was recreated. By June, 1781 the men were organized into three tiny battalions. On January 5, 1783 a shortage of supplies in the area of operations led to the reduction of the North Carolina Continentals to one regiment of about two hundred men,[182] some of whom were enlisted for only eighteen months. Between May 26, 1783 and August 18, 1783 the last of these men were furloughed and on November 15, 1783 discharged.

2nd North Carolina Regiment of 1775   This unit had a history the same as the 1st North Carolina Regiment of 1775 (which see).
>   COMMANDER: Colonel Robert Howe September 1, 1775-March, 1776.

2nd North Carolina Regiment of 1776   This regiment had a record identical to that of the 1st North Carolina Regiment of 1776 (which see).
>   COMMANDERS: Colonel Alexander Martin April 10, 1776-November 22, 1777.
>   Colonel John Patten November 22, 1777-1780.

2nd North Carolina Regiment of 1780   Service identical to the 1st North Carolina Regiment of 1780 (which see).

2nd North Carolina Regiment of 1781   This regiment had a history very similar to the 1st North Carolina Regiment of 1781 (which see). Its men were incorporated into the 1st North Carolina on January 5, 1783.

3rd North Carolina Regiment of 1776   This regiment was one of four that was apparently created in April, 1776 and accepted by Congress May 7, 1776. The regiment served in its home state in 1776, then was reorganized and sent north to join the Main Army where it served until 1779 when it was brought south and completely reorganized in late 1779 and early 1780. *See* 1st North Carolina Regiment of 1780.

COMMANDERS: Colonel Jethro Sumner April 15, 1776-January 9, 1779.
Lieutenant Colonel Henry Dixon January 9, 1779-June 20, 1779.
Lieutenant Colonel Robert McLane June 7, 1779-1780.

3rd North Carolina Regiment of 1780   This unit had a history the same as the 1st North Carolina Regiment of 1780 (which see).

3rd North Carolina Regiment of 1781   This regiment had a history very similar to the 2nd North Carolina Regiment of 1781 (which see).

4th North Carolina Regiment of 1776   This regiment was also created in April, 1776 and accepted into the Continental service on May 7, 1776. It served within the state during 1776, then was reorganized and sent to join the Main Army. On May 29, 1778 the understrength regiment's enlisted men were incorporated into the more senior three North Carolina regiments and the officers of the 4th North Carolina together with those of the 5th and 6th Regiments were sent back to the state with instructions to recruit four battalions of Continentals who were to serve for only nine months. From this date the regiment ceased to exist as an actual formation.
COMMANDER: Colonel Thomas Polk April 16, 1776-June 28, 1778.

4th North Carolina Regiment of 1779   This was a temporary regiment created in the spring of 1779 using mostly furloughed Continentals who had been persuaded to return for nine months and a few militia who volunteered for sixteen months. The corps disappeared at the end of 1779.

4th North Carolina Regiment of 1782   On February 6, 1782 the North Carolina Line was reorganized on paper as four regiments. This paper reorganization actually exerted little influence on North Carolina units in the field. There were actually elements of three regiments in the field at this time, but the 4th Regiment never existed at all except on paper.

5th North Carolina Regiment of 1776   This regiment had a history identical to the 4th North Carolina Regiment (which see).

COMMANDER: Colonel Edward Buncombe April 15, 1776-October 19, 1777.

5th North Carolina Regiment of 1779   This regiment had a history identical to that of the 4th North Carolina Regiment of 1779 (which see).

6th North Carolina Regiment   This regiment had a history identical to the 4th North Carolina Regiment (which see).
COMMANDERS: Colonel John Lillington April 15, 1776-May 6, 1776.
Major Gideon Lamb May 6, 1776-1778. Promoted to colonel January 26, 1777.

7th North Carolina Regiment   This regiment was created on November 26, 1776 to help fill the state's quota for 1777 as specified in September, 1776. The unit was recruited in a very haphazard manner and by Congressional action of May, 1778 its few officers were to join the officers sent back home from the Main Army to recruit. After this date the regiment, such as it was, became defunct. *See* 1st North Carolina Regiment of 1776.
COMMANDER: Colonel James Hogun November 26, 1776-1778.

8th North Carolina Regiment   This regiment had a history nearly identical to the 7th North Carolina Regiment (which see).
COMMANDER: Colonel James Armstrong November 26, 1776-June 1, 1778.

9th North Carolina Regiment   This unit had a history nearly identical to the 7th North Carolina Regiment (which see). Its colonel was not even appointed until April, 1777.
COMMANDER: Colonel John P. Williams April 7, 1777-June 1, 1778.

10th North Carolina Regiment   The 10th North Carolina was raised on state initiative in April, 1777 and later, in June, accepted by Congress. In early 1778 the regiment joined the Main Army and along with the 1st through 3rd Regiments was to remain intact in the reorganization of the North Carolina Continentals of May,

1778, but the regiment was so understrength that it was soon incorporated into the three senior regiments of the North Carolina Line.
    COMMANDER: Colonel Abraham Shepard April 17, 1777-June 1, 1778.

Northern Army   After 1775 the troops serving in the Canadian theatre of operations were generally called the Northern Army. After the victory at Saratoga in 1777 the Northern Army gradually faded into insignificance and finally disappeared altogether around mid-1783.

Northern Department   The Northern Department was a de facto military administrative district established in June or July, 1776. Its boundaries may be loosely defined as extending along the northern and western frontiers of Massachusetts, New Hampshire, Connecticut claims, and New York. The department's supply lines reached into the heart of New England.

O

Baron Ottendorf's Independent Company   On December 5, 1776
Congress commissioned Baron Ottendorf, a foreigner, to raise an
independent corps in the Continental Army. The whole idea was
somewhat ridiculous. Washington had employed commando-type
forces previously with some success, but they had been Americans,
led by Americans, not a miscreant force of mercenaries that Americans of some military knowledge must have known a unit formed by
a soldier of German extraction implied, a "freikorps" of foreign
scoundrels. Ottendorf's corps was to consist of himself as major
and commander of a light infantry company consisting of 2 lieutenants and 60 other ranks and also two companies of "hunters"
(riflemen?) each of 1 captain, 2 lieutenants, and 45 other ranks. An
adjutant who was to serve as paymaster and quartermaster was also
authorized to bring the corps up to 160 men on paper.[183] On
December 7, 1776 Ottendorf was given command of the men
previously raised by Captain Schott for an independent company
planned earlier. Ottendorf's Corps had difficulty in completing itself properly and on June 11, 1777 Washington replaced Ottendorf
with Lieutenant Colonel Armand. As Armand's Legion (which
see) the corps went on to gain considerable fame (or infamy).
     COMMANDER: Major Nicholas Dietrich, Baron de Ottendorf.

P

Partisan Corps   A body of special troops intended for raiding and reconnaissance. Armand's Legion, Lee's Legion, and Pulaski's Legion were all sometimes referred to as partisan corps. In October, 1780 it was decided that two of the partisan corps, Lee's and Armand's, should be retained. Each was to have three horse and three foot troops, each troop of 50 men. Some modern writers, basing themselves on this Congressional resolve, refer to Lee's and Armand's as the 1st and 2nd Partisan Corps. Heitman's list of officers of the Continental Army also posthumously bestows the designation of 3rd Partisan Corps on Pulaski's Legion.

Colonel Patton's Additional Continental Regiment   Patton's Regiment was authorized January 11, 1777. Some Marylanders served in the regiment. By Congressional order of January 13, 1779 the regiment was broken up, Captain Allen McLane's Delaware company going into the Delaware Regiment and the other companies being turned over to the new 11th Pennsylvania Regiment.

    COMMANDERS: Colonel John Patton January 11, 1777-February 3, 1778.

                     Lieutenant Colonel John Park February 3, 1778-October 29, 1778.

                     Major Joseph Prowell October 29, 1778-January 13, 1779.

Pennsylvania Hussar Company

Pennsylvania Hussar Company   Bills for the equipment of a hussar company raising in Pennsylvania appear in the records of the Continental Congress during the summer of 1775. The author has yet to find mention of anyone who served in this unit. It is possible that the bills are for the Philadelphia City Troop of Light Horse, an elite volunteer militia unit that often rendered services to the Congress without pay. It is recorded that the Hussars offered their services to Congress and were accepted, but were never called to serve, at least not under the title of Hussars.

1st Pennsylvania Battalion of 1776   On November 25, 1775 Congress took the infantry battalion then raising in Pennsylvania into the Continental service. The battalion had first been planned in mid-October. The battalion was ordered to consist after January 4, 1776 of seven line companies and one rifle company.[184] The unit was ordered mustered in on February 13. The battalion served through the year, being completely reorganized over the winter of 1776-77. It provided the organizational basis for the new 2nd Pennsylvania Regiment.

COMMANDERS: Colonel John Bull November 25, 1775-January 22, 1776.
Colonel John P. De Haas January 22, 1776-October 25, 1776.

1st Pennsylvania Regiment of 1777   The 1st Pennsylvania was created over the winter of 1776-77 from new recruits and Pennsylvania Continental veterans. Elements of the regiment served on until January, 1783, but after 1780 the regiment, itself, was not a viable tactical or administrative entity. *See* 1st Pennsylvania Battalion of 1781.

COMMANDERS: Colonel Edward Hand January 1, 1777-April 1, 1777.
Colonel James Chambers April 12, 1777-January 17, 1781.
Colonel Daniel Brodhead January 17, 1781-November 3, 1783.

1st Pennsylvania Battalion of 1781   In 1781 the men of the six remaining Pennsylvania regiments were formed into three battalions for the campaign in the Southern Department. After January 1, 1783 these battalions were all that remained of the Pennsylvania Line as the officers not in them were retired, deactivating the old six regiment structure for good. The last men in these battalions were apparently furloughed in June and July, 1783 and discharged on November 3 of that year.

COMMANDER: Colonel Walter Stewart (?)

2nd Pennsylvania Battalion of 1776   On December 15, 1775 Congress decided to raise four more Continental battalions in Pennsylvania. On January 3, 1776 the field officers for the battalions were elected by Congress. On January 4, 1776 it was resolved that each battalion should have seven line companies and one rifle company. This organization with an odd number of line companies was bitterly protested by many officers. On February 13, 1776 the unit was ordered mustered. The battalion served through the year until the change of enlistment policy led to its reorganization over the winter of 1776-77 as the 3rd Pennsylvania Regiment.

COMMANDERS: Colonel Arthur St. Clair January 3, 1776-August 9, 1776.
Colonel Joseph Wood September 7, 1776-?

2nd Pennsylvania Regiment of 1777   The organizational history of this regiment was very similar to that of the 1st Pennsylvania Regiment of 1777 (which see).

COMMANDERS: Colonel John P. De Haas October 25, 1776-February 21, 1777.
Colonel James Irvine March 12, 1777-June 1, 1777.
Colonel Henry Bicker June 6, 1777-July 1, 1778.
Colonel Walter Stewart July 1, 1778-January 1, 1783.

2nd Pennsylvania Battalion of 1781   This battalion apparently had an organizational history similar to the 1st Pennsylvania Battalion of 1781 (which see).

COMMANDER: Colonel Richard Butler (?)

3rd Pennsylvania Battalion of 1776   This battalion had an organizational history almost identical to the 2nd Pennsylvania Battalion of 1776 (which see). It was reorganized over the winter of 1776-77 as the 4th Pennsylvania Regiment.

COMMANDERS: Colonel John Shee January 3, 1776-September 27, 1776.

Lieutenant Colonel Lambert Cadwalader September 27, 1776-November 16, 1776.

3rd Pennsylvania Regiment of 1777   The organizational history of this regiment was very similar to that of the 1st Pennsylvania Regiment of 1777 (which see).

COMMANDERS: Colonel Joseph Wood September 7, 1776-July 31, 1777.
Colonel Thomas Craig August 1, 1777-January 1, 1783.

3rd Pennsylvania Battalion of 1781   This battalion apparently had an organizational history similar to the 1st Pennsylvania Battalion of 1781 (which see).

COMMANDER: Colonel Thomas Craig (?)

4th Pennsylvania Battalion of 1776   This regiment had an organizational history almost identical to the 2nd Pennsylvania Battalion of 1776 (which see). This unit is known to have had a light company armed with rifles. The battalion was reorganized over the winter of 1776-77 as the 5th Pennsylvania Regiment.

COMMANDER: Colonel Anthony Wayne January 3, 1776-c. November, 1776.

4th Pennsylvania Regiment of 1777   The organizational history of this regiment was very similar to that of the 1st Pennsylvania Regiment of 1777 (which see).

COMMANDER: Colonel Lambert Cadwalader October 25, 1776-January 22, 1779.
Lieutenant Colonel William Butler January 22, 1779-January 1, 1783.

5th Pennsylvania Battalion of 1776   This regiment had an organizational history almost identical to the 2nd Pennsylvania Battalion of 1776 (which see). It was reorganized over the winter of 1776-77 as the 6th Pennsylvania Regiment.

COMMANDER: Colonel Robert Magaw January 3, 1776-c. November, 1776.

5th Pennsylvania Regiment of 1777   The organizational history of this regiment was very similar to that of the 1st Pennsylvania Regiment of 1777 (which see).

COMMANDER: Colonel Francis Johnston c. November, 1776-
January 17, 1781.
Colonel Richard Butler January 17, 1781-
January 1, 1783.

6th Pennsylvania Battalion of 1776   On January 10, 1776 this battalion was created by Congress. It served through the year and was reorganized over the winter of 1776-77 as the 7th Pennsylvania Regiment.

COMMANDER: Colonel William Irvine January 10, 1776-c. November, 1776.

6th Pennsylvania Regiment of 1777   The organizational history of this regiment was very similar to that of the 1st Pennsylvania Regiment of 1777 (which see).

COMMANDERS: Colonel Robert Magaw c. November, 1776-
January 17, 1781.
Colonel Richard Humpton January 17, 1781-
January 1, 1783.

7th Pennsylvania Regiment   The 7th Pennsylvania was organized from veterans and new recruits over the winter of 1776-77 and served until January 17, 1781 when it was disbanded to comply with General Orders from Washington.

COMMANDERS: Colonel William Irvine c. November, 1776-
May 12, 1779.
Lieutenant Colonel Morgan Conner May 12,
1779-January, 1780.
Major James Parr January, 1780-August 9,
1780.
Lieutenant Colonel Josiah Harmar August 9,
1780-January 17, 1781.

8th Pennsylvania Regiment   The regiment was created on October 25, 1776 as part of Pennsylvania's expanded quota. It served until January 17, 1781 when it was broken up in compliance with General Orders.

COMMANDERS: Colonel Aenas Makay October 25, 1776-
February 14, 1777.
Colonel Daniel Brodhead March 12, 1777-
January 17, 1781.

9th Pennsylvania Regiment   This regiment had an organizational history almost identical to the 8th Pennsylvania Regiment (which see).

COMMANDERS: Colonel James Irvine October 25, 1776-March 12, 1777.
Colonel Anthony Morris March 12, 1777-June 7, 1777.
Colonel Richard Butler June 7, 1777-January 17, 1781.

10th Pennsylvania Regiment   This regiment had an organizational history almost identical to the 8th Pennsylvania Regiment (which see).

COMMANDERS: Colonel Joseph Pinrose October 25, 1776-February 7, 1777.
Colonel James Chambers March 12, 1777-April 12, 1777.
Colonel George Nagel February 7, 1777-July 1, 1778.
Colonel Richard Humpton July 1, 1778-January 17, 1781.

11th Pennsylvania Regiment of 1777   The 11th Pennsylvania was created on October 25, 1776 and served until it was merged into the 10th Pennsylvania on July 1, 1778.

COMMANDERS: Colonel Richard Humpton October 25, 1776-July 1, 1778.

11th Pennsylvania Regiment of 1779   On December 16, 1778 it was decided to reorganize Hartley's Additional Continental Regiment (which see) as a new 11th Pennsylvania Regiment. This was done and the new 11th served until January, 1781.

COMMANDERS: Colonel Thomas Hartley December 16, 1778-February 13, 1779.
Lieutenant Colonel Morgan Connor February 13, 1779-May 12, 1779.
Lieutenant Colonel Adam Hubley May 13, 1779-January 17, 1781.

12th Pennsylvania Regiment   The 12th Pennsylvania Regiment was created October 25, 1776 and served until July 1, 1778 when it was incorporated into the 6th Pennsylvania Regiment.

COMMANDER: Colonel William Cooke September 28, 1776-
March 7, 1778. Commission predated.
Lieutenant Colonel Neigel Gray March 7,
1778-June 2, 1778.

13th Pennsylvania Regiment   This regiment was originally the non-
Continental Pennsylvania State Regiment organized in the spring of
1777 under Colonel Bull. On November 12, 1777 Congress voted
to adopt it as the 13th Pennsylvania. The regiment was merged into
the 2nd Pennsylvania on July 1, 1778.   ˋ
COMMANDER: Colonel Walter Stewart November 12, 1777-
July 1, 1778.

Pennsylvania Rifle Regiment   On June 14, 1775 Congress resolved
that Pennsylvania should raise six companies of riflemen who were
to be paid by the Continental Congress. Each company was to consist of 1 captain, 3 lieutenants, 4 sergeants, 4 corporals, 1 drummer
or trumpeter, and 68 privates. On June 22 Congress authorized two
more Pennsylvania rifle companies and further planned that the
eight companies should be formed into a battalion. Accordingly
William Thompson was appointed colonel and a lieutenant colonel
and a major were also named.[185] By the end of July the battalion
was formed. Later it was joined by a ninth company raised in
Lancaster County, Pennsylvania. The battalion served with Continental Army around Boston, part of it being detached for the Canadian invasion. The regiment was reorganized over the winter of
1775-76 as the 1st Continental Regiment. Several sources state the
regiment was rearmed gradually with muskets and converted into an
ordinary infantry battalion, but the author has yet to find contemporary documentation of this. Late in the year 1776 the regiment
seems to have been the nucleus of the 1st Pennsylvania Regiment of
the reorganizing Pennsylvania Line.
COMMANDERS: Colonel William Thompson June 25, 1775-
March 1, 1776.
Colonel Edward Hand March 7, 1776-
December 31, 1776. Hand was lieutenant colonel of the regiment until March 7.

Pennsylvania Riflemen   One June 24, 1781 the state of Pennsylvania
was requested by Washington to find a force of 300 riflemen (six
companies each of 50 men under a captain and two subalterns) to

be commanded by a major. Major Parr was recommended for the command.[186] The unit was to serve for a short term and be paid by Congress. The riflemen were raised sometime after July 16 and served with distinction in the Yorktown campaign after which they were sent home.

Philadelphia Associators　As organized in 1775 the Philadelphia Associators consisted of three line battalions each of about nine musketeer and one light company, a rifle company, and the Philadelphia City Troop of Light Horse. This was the civic militia of the Philadelphia area.

The Philadelphia Associators consisted in 1776 of four line battalions and a rifle battalion organized by volunteers from the militia of the Philadelphia area. Under Acting Brigadier General Cadwalader they joined Washington's army in the closing days of 1776 and participated in the Trenton-Princeton campaign. Each line battalion had a light company and during the campaign the light companies and Captain Thomas Rodney's Light Company of the Dover County, Delaware Militia were formed into a light battalion under Captain George Henry.

Philadelphia City Troop of Light Horse　This troop of calvalry with 3 officers and 22 other ranks was formed in 1774 from Philadelphia gentlemen of property as a volunteer militia unit. So far as known, the troop never accepted a penny from Congress for its services during the war. These services included escort duties and dispatch carrying for the Continental government and also service in the field at Trenton and Princeton in the winter of 1776-77 and also briefly in several later campaigns. The well mounted troop was an excellent reconnaissance force. A unit of the Pennsylvania National Guard still upholds the traditions and name of the old City Troop.

Corps of Pioneers　On March 26, 1782 Congress authorized a corps of thirty pioneers to be enlisted in the Southern Army for one year.[187] No further information.

Fort Pitt and Fort Randolph Independent Companies　On January 8, 1777 Congress decided to garrison Fort Pitt and Fort Randolph each with an independent company of 1 captain, 2 lieutenants, 1 ensign, and 100 enlisted men.[188] These companies were raised in Virginia sometime after February, 1777. Although these companies were not liable for service away from their forts, most of their members joined the 12th Virginia when it marched north in April of 1777. The companies were apparently reorganized using men from the Virginia State Troops. In July, 1779 both companies were in garrison at Fort Pitt. The company commanders in 1777 were Captains Robert Campbell and John Robinson. In 1779 the company commanders were Captains Henry Heth and James O'Hara.

Provost Corps　　*See* Captain Von Heer's Provost Troop of Light Dragoons

Pulaski's Legion　　On March 28, 1778 Brigadier General Count Pulaski was authorized by Congress to raise an independent corps of 68 cavalrymen and 200 light infantrymen. Pulaski, who had been the nominal commander of the Brigade of Continental Calvary, was apparently very restless as the figurehead leader of two or three hundred rag-tag troopers in four regiments so short of men, horses, and supplies that they could not even be gathered together for him to command, so desperately were they foraging for subsistence.

Pulaski doubtlessly wanted out of this muddle and he was eager to fight. Washington was probably only too glad to be rid of the strange foreigner. Pulaski procured handsome uniforms for his corps, lances for his horsemen (and unless the Congressional records contain a misprint—for the footmen as well[189]), and set about to obtain men. Some recruits were obtained in Maryland. General Washington had allowed Pulaski to recruit up to a third of his infantry from German deserters, but Pulaski recruited anyone who came forward in the true "freikorps" tradition. There were British deserters among the cavalry, much to Washington's displeasure.[190] As Pulaski's Legion was actually organized in the autumn of 1778 it consisted of a staff, three troops of calvary, one company of riflemen (chasseurs), a grenadier company, two infantry companies, and a "supernumerary" company. A British source also credited it with a detachment of artillery armed with a light brass field gun. Each company and troop consisted of about 25 or 30 men. Pulaski attempted to christen his corps the Maryland Legion but this name was seldom used.

February 2, 1779 Congress ordered Pulaski's Legion to the Southern Department to which it proceeded, frightening the local populations along the way with its poor conduct. October 11, 1779 Pulaski died from a terrible wound received in an attempt to retake

Savannah. On December 29, 1779 Congress authorized the survivors of his corps to be disbanded, which General Lincoln did, the cavalry going into the 1st Light Dragoon Regiment, the infantry being reassigned to the 1st South Carolina Regiment.[191] The date of ultimate disbandment is somewhat of a mystery, but it was sometime between December, 1779 and April, 1780. Almost all these men were captured at Charleston on May 12, 1780. What to do with the officers of Pulaski's Legion was more difficult to decide than the disposition of the men, but on November 7, 1780 Congress finally decided to incorporate them into Armand's Legion.[192]

COMMANDERS: Brigadier General Kasimir Pulaski March 28, 1778-October 11, 1779

Major Peter Vernier October, 1779- April 14, 1780 (?)

Q

Quartermaster Artificers *See* Staff Departments, Quartermaster
Department.

R

Fort Randolph Independent Company   *See* Fort Pitt and Fort Randolph Independent Companies.

Rangers   Rangers were largely frontier troops. Their primary function was to range up and down the vast western frontiers of the states gathering information and conducting hit and run raids when necessary to keep the enemy off balance. Most rangers were required to furnish their own weapons which might be anything from rifles to sabers, shotguns to knives. Sometimes they were mounted.

Captain Samuel Ransom's Independent Company   Ransom's company between August 26, 1776 and June 23, 1778 had an organizational history virtually identical to Durkee's company (which see).

Rawlings' Additional Continental Regiment   On January 12, 1777 Moses Rawlings was appointed colonel of one of the sixteen additional Continental regiments Washington was authorized to raise. Rawlings, a Marylander, as lieutenant colonel of Stephenson's Maryland and Virginia Rifle Regiment (which see) had been captured at Fort Washington the previous fall. Washington apparently intended that Rawlings, after his exchange, should reorganize the remnants of the regiment and reraise it. This was not to be.

In February, 1777 five companies intended for the corps were drafted into the 11th Virginia Regiment.[193] Further recruiting did not go smoothly. On January 23, 1779 Rawlings was instructed to raise three companies and go to Fort Pitt, but a short time afterwards Washington wrote that Colonel Rawlings had only 70 men and that raising the three companies was hopeless.[194] On April 8, 1779 Rawlings' Rifle Corps was ordered incorporated into the German Battalion.[195] This was more than Rawlings could take. He resigned sometime after May 11 of that year and the pitiful remnants of his corps merged with the remnants of the German Battalion to form the so called Maryland Corps (which see).[196]

COMMANDER: Colonel Moses Rawlings January 12, 1777-c. May, 1779.

1st Rhode Island Regiment of 1775   In late April, 1775 the Rhode Island legislature decided to raise 1,500 men to observe the British forces in Boston and defend the colony. These men were to be paid by Rhode Island and were to swear allegiance to the King of England. Accordingly a brigade of three regiments was created. Each regiment was to have 1 colonel, 1 lieutenant colonel, 1 major, 1 adjutant, 1 quartermaster, 1 surgeon, 1 surgeon's mate, and eight companies. Each company was to have 1 captain or captain lieutenant, 1 lieutenant, 1 ensign, and about 60 privates. This regiment was accordingly recruited in May from the militia of King's and Kent Counties.[197] On June 14, 1775 this regiment was among the New England army taken into the pay of Congress. June 28, 1775 the colony's legislature voted to increase the size of each regiment to twelve companies.[198] The regiment served until December, 1775 when it disbanded, some of its personnel going into the 9th or 11th Continental Regiments.

COMMANDER: Colonel James Varnum May 3, 1775-December, 1775.

1st Rhode Island Regiment of 1777   The second regiment to bear this number was organized in late 1776 and early 1777 and served until the Rhode Island Continentals were reorganized in the first part of 1781. There were a great many Negro soldiers in this regiment during its last years.

COMMANDER: Colonel James Varnum January 1, 1777-February 27, 1777.
Colonel Christopher Greene February 27, 1777-May 14, 1781.

2nd Rhode Island Regiment of 1775   This regiment had a history similar to the 1st Rhode Island Regiment of 1775 (which see). It was recruited from the militia of Providence County.

COMMANDER: Colonel Daniel Hitchcock May 3, 1775-December, 1775.

2nd Rhode Island Regiment of 1777   The second regiment of this number had a history similar to the 1st Rhode Island Regiment of 1777 (which see).

COMMANDER: Colonel Daniel Hitchcock January 1, 1777-January 13, 1777.

Colonel Israel Angell January 13, 1777-January 1, 1781.

3rd Rhode Island Regiment   This regiment had a history similar to the 1st Rhode Island Regiment of 1775 (which see). Included among the regiment's original eight companies was a company of the Rhode Island Train of Artillery (which see). The other men came from the militia of Newport and Bristol Counties.

COMMANDER:.   Colonel Thomas Church May 3, 1775-December, 1775.

Rhode Island Regiment   During the first part of 1781 the two Rhode Island regiments were completely reorganized into one regiment. The regiment served at Yorktown and after June 12, 1783 the new recruits of this regiment were among the men retained until November 3-5, 1783 when the regiment was discharged.

COMMANDER: Lieutenant Colonel Jeremiah Olney May 14, 1781-November 3, 1783.

Rhode Island Garrison Regiments   In the spring of 1776 two regiments of Rhode Island state troops were taken into the Continental pay for several months. They were not, however, actually Continental troops.

Rhode Island Train of Artillery   One of the few well trained and equipped militia units when the revolution began in 1775. The company was assigned (or at least volunteers from it were) to the 3rd Rhode Island Regiment when that colony mobilized. (*See* 3rd Rhode Island Regiment.) After May 3 there is evidence that it was incorporated into Gridley's Massachusetts Artillery Regiment (which see).

Captain Bernard Roman's Independent Artillery Company   This company was raised in Pennsylvania after February 8, 1776 for the Continental service. In December command passed to Gibbs Jones. By the plan of January 8, 1778 the company became part of the 4th Battalion of Continental Artillery.

S

Corps of Sappers and Miners   *See* Engineer's Department.

Savannah Artillery Company   *See* Captain Lee's Independent Artillery Company.

Captain John Paul Schott's Independent Corps   Schott was appointed captain of an independent Pennsylvania company 150 strong on September 6, 1776. On December 7, 1776 his men were taken into Ottendorf's Company.

Captain James Scott's Volunteer Company   On January 18, 1777 a company of volunteers from the Virginia militia of Farquier County offered their services for three months and were accepted. The company had 1 captain, 2 lieutenants, 1 ensign, 4 sergeants, 4 corporals, 1 drummer, 1 fifer, and 64 privates.[199]

Separate Army   The so called Separate Army was created on June 16, 1775 to secure the Canadian frontier.[200] Its officers were commissioned by Congress and thus the Separate Army should be considered a part of what was to become known as the Continental Army. By the end of the year the term "Northern Army" (which see) had largely replaced the use of Separate Army to designate these forces.

Colonel Seymour's Connecticut Light Horse   In early July, 1776 a regiment of 400 Connecticut mounted men offered their services to General Washington and the Continental cause. They were accepted, but then on July 16 the general dismissed them.[201] Washington maintained that the exemption from fatigue duty that the men desired so as to be able to take care of their horses was unwarranted. The sense of this decision has been argued by historians for years, some claiming the horsemen would have provided valuable reconnaissance, others saying the men and horses were simply not up to field work and that their equipment was wretched. The fact remains they were sent home.

Colonel Sherburne's Additional Continental Regiment   Created January 12, 1777, this regiment seems to have had adequate training, supplies, and men. Sherburne's Regiment included three companies from Connecticut and a number of Maryland men. On May 1, 1780 the regiment broke up, many of the men going into Samuel B. Webb's Regiment.

COMMANDER: Colonel Henry Sherburne January 12, 1777-May 1, 1780.

Smallwood's Maryland Regiment   January 14, 1776 the Maryland legislature created an armed force. It was maintained by the State of Maryland but was, according to the act that created it, available for service not only for the State of Maryland, but also the Continental cause. Smallwood's Regiment was created on January 14 as a unit of eight line companies and a light company of riflemen. Each company had 1 captain, 2 lieutenants, 1 ensign, and 68 privates. On July 17, 1776 Smallwood was directed by Congress to take his troops from the Flying Camp (which see) to join the Main Army and place himself under Washington's command.[202] This he did. Part of the regiment made the march to New York mounted, but during the campaign in New York the regiment served exclusively in the infantry role for which it was intended.

Although any specific legislation making Smallwood's a Continental unit is today unavailable, it seems that at least from the time it joined Washington it was regarded as Continental. At any rate on January 8, 1777, Smallwood's Battalion was voted to be paid off by Congress,[203] thus implying Continental service. After the one-year men left, those who remained from the regiment formed the cadre of the 1st Maryland Regiment of 1777 (which see) in the reorganized Continental Army.

COMMANDER: Colonel William Smallwood January 14, 1776-December, 1776.

Independent South Carolina Artillery Companies   February 22, 1776 two independent companies each of 100 men and one of 60 men were authorized by the South Carolina Provincial Congress to man coastal batteries at Charleston, Beaufort, and Georgetown.[204] These were volunteer companies. By February, 1779 the Charleston Company had become a battalion of two companies under Major Grimball. (Charleston referred to as Charles Town in early documents)
COMMANDERS: Captain T. Grimball (Charleston)
Captain Wm. Harden (Beaufort)
Captain Paul Trapier (Georgetown)

South Carolina Artillery Regiment   *See* 4th South Carolina Regiment.

South Carolina Light Dragoons   *See* 3rd South Carolina Regiment of 1775; Horry's Light Dragoons.

1st South Carolina Regiment of 1775   June 6, 1775 the Provincial Congress of South Carolina authorized two regiments of foot and one of rangers to be raised in the state and placed under the direction of the Continental Congress. Each of the foot regiments was to have 1 colonel, 1 lieutenant colonel, 1 major, 1 adjutant, 1 quartermaster, 1 surgeon, 2 surgeon's mates, 1 sergeant major, 1 armorer, 1 assistant armorer, 5 extra privates, and ten companies (apparently including one of grenadiers). Each company was to have 1 captain, 2 lieutenants, 3 sergeants, 3 corporals, 2 drummers, and 69 privates.[205] The 1st South Carolina was accordingly raised and equipped by the state. On November 4, 1775 the Continental Congress voted to support three battalions in South Carolina, thus confirming the Continental status the regiment always claimed for itself.[206] On February 22, 1776 a quartermaster sergeant was authorized for the regiment. The regiment's men fought bravely in defense of Charleston that year. September 20, 1776 the regiment was officially turned over to the Continental Congress. South Carolina Continentals seem to have been rather out of touch with organizational changes further north in the next years. In May, 1778 Congress ordered all South Carolina regiments merged into one,[207] but this was not done, nor were Congressional plans for the internal organization of regiments followed. As late as August of 1778 the regiment had ten companies including one of grenadiers.[208] Finally, around the beginning of 1780, General Lincoln actually reorganized the South Carolina Continentals. *(See* 1st South Carolina Regiment of 1780.)

> COMMANDERS: Colonel Christopher Gadsen June 17, 1775-September 16, 1776.
> Colonel Charles Pinckney September 16, 1776-1780.

1st South Carolina Regiment of 1780   In late 1779 and early 1780 the South Carolina Continentals were reorganized into three small regiments of infantry and one of artillery. The infantry regiments each had eight line companies and one light company.[209] The infantry remnants of Pulaski's Legion were absorbed into the 1st Regiment. This regiment was captured at Charleston on May 12, 1780.

> COMMANDER: Colonel Charles Pinckney

1st South Carolina Regiment of 1782   In October, 1780 Congress set South Carolina's quota of Continental troops at two battalions. Theoretically they should have been commanded by Colonels Charles Pinckney and Francis Marion respectively, but Pinckney was a prisoner and Marion was leading a harried existence in the swamps with his partisans at this time so these two battalions were not raised. In the summer of 1782 some recruiting of Continental infantry and artillery may have occurred. Not over 80 men were ever enlisted. Between December, 1782 and November 15, 1783 these men were all furloughed and discharged.

2nd South Carolina Regiment of 1775   This regiment was created on June 6, 1775 by the South Carolina Provincial Congress and had a service record almost identical in all respects to the 1st South Carolina Regiment of 1775 (which see).

> COMMANDERS: Colonel William Moultrie June 17, 1775-September 16, 1776.
> Colonel Isaac Motte September 16, 1776-1780.

2nd South Carolina Regiment of 1780   This unit was also a result of the 1779-1780 reorganization of the South Carolina Continentals.

It was captured at Charleston May 12, 1780. *See* 1st South Carolina Regiment of 1780.

COMMANDER: Colonel Isaac Motte

2nd South Carolina Regiment of 1782   *See* 1st South Carolina Regiment of 1782.

3rd South Carolina Regiment (Mounted Rangers)   On June 6, 1775 the Provincial Congress of South Carolina voted to raise a regiment of rangers who were to be placed under the direction of the Continental Congress. The regiment was to be mounted and was to have 1 lieutenant colonel, 1 major, 1 surgeon, 1 paymaster, and nine companies each of 1 captain, 2 lieutenants, 2 sergeants, 1 drummer, and 50 corporals and privates.[210] On February 21, 1776 it was voted to allow the regiment an adjutant and a quartermaster. A move to convert the regiment to dragoons was voted down and it was voted to equip the regiment with rifles. It is questionable whether many of the mounted rangers actually obtained rifles. On July 24, 1776 the Continental Congress definitely accepted the rangers for Continental service[211] and on September 20 the regiment was turned over to Congress. The organization for the rangers decreed by the Continental Congress was 1 lieutenant colonel commandant, 1 major, 1 paymaster, 1 surgeon, and ten companies each of 1 captain, 2 lieutenants, two sergeants, and 50 privates. The regiment existed until the 1779-1780 reorganization of the South Carolina Continentals.

COMMANDER: Lieutenant Colonel William Thomson June 17, 1775-1780.

3rd South Carolina Regiment of 1780   The exact date this regiment was created and its composition are not mentioned. Probably it was created in late 1779 or early 1780 when the South Carolina Continentals were reorganized. It was certainly the result of this reorganization and not the old mounted rangers of the former 3rd South Carolina although some of its men may have served in that unit formerly. This regiment was surrendered at Charleston on May 12, 1780.

COMMANDER: ?

4th South Carolina Regiment (Artillery)   On November 12, 1775 the South Carolina Provincial Congress voted to raise an artillery regiment, primarily to man the coastal batteries in their state. It is evident, however, that South Carolina considered the troops as in the Continental service and expected them to be paid by Continental funds. On June 18, 1776 the Continental Congress voted to take the South Carolina Artillery Regiment into its service and the regiment entered Continental service September 20, 1776. As originally planned the regiment was to have consisted of 1 lieutenant colonel commandant, 1 major, 1 adjutant, 1 quartermaster, 1 paymaster, 1 surgeon, 1 surgeon's mate, 1 sergeant workman, 1 armorer, 1 assistant armorer, 2 extra privates, and three companies each of 1 captain, 2 lieutenants, 2 lieutenant-fireworkers, 4 sergeants, 4 corporals, 1 drummer, 1 fifer, 10 gunners, and 42 privates.[212] About 1779 the regiment was increased to six companies. The regiment was among those that surrendered at Charleston on May 12, 1780. At that time it numbered around 100 men. In 1782 there may have been some attempt to reform the South Carolina Artillery.

COMMANDERS: Lieutenant Colonel Owen Roberts Commission dated September 16, 1776-June 20, 1779.

Colonel Barnard Beekman June 20, 1779-1780.

5th South Carolina Regiment (1st South Carolina Rifles) On February 21, 1776 the Provincial Congress voted to create a regiment of expert riflemen which was to serve until June 1, 1777. The rifle regiment was to have field officers, an adjutant, a quartermaster, a paymaster, a surgeon, a sergeant major, a quartermaster sergeant, and seven companies. Each company was to have 1 captain, 2 lieutenants, 1 ensign, 4 sergeants, 4 corporals, and 92 riflemen.[213] On March 25, 1776 this regiment was accepted for Continental service and on September 20, 1776 it was turned over to Continental command. The regiment's term of service was extended and it remained until broken up over the winter of 1779-1780.

COMMANDERS: Colonel Isaac Huger Commission dated September 16, 1776-January 9, 1777.

Lieutenant Colonel Alexander McIntosh January, 1777-1780.

6th South Carolina Regiment (2nd South Carolina Rifles) This corps was authorized by the Provincial Congress on February 28, 1776 as one lieutenant colonel commandant, one major, and five companies.[214] On September 20, 1776 the regiment was placed under Continental control. The regiment broke up in the winter of 1779-1780.

COMMANDER: Lieutenant Colonel Thomas Sumter

Southern Army   The Southern Army might be said to date from February 27, 1776 when a major general, three brigadier generals, and a staff were created to command the troops in the service of Congress in the Southern Department. The Southern Army was disbanded November 15, 1783.

Southern Department   On February 27, 1776 the Southern Department was established by Congress as a military administrative district comprising Virginia, North Carolina, South Carolina, and Georgia.[215]

Captain Spaulding's Independent Company   This was an independent Continental Company formed June 23, 1778 under Spaulding by merging Durkee's and Ransom's companies (which see).It was garrisoned in the Wyoming area during most of 1779-1780. On January 1, 1781 it was broken up and its men assigned to the 1st Connecticut Regiment.[216]

Colonel Spencer's Additional Continental Regiment   Created January 15, 1777, Oliver Spencer's Regiment was raised mostly in New Jersey. On April 22, 1779 Malcolm's Additional Regiment was ordered to merge with it. The regiment seems to have been called the 5th New Jersey Regiment for a time (1777 to mid-1778). The regiment was broken up in General Orders of November 1, 1780 effective January 1, 1781.

Staff Departments

ADJUTANT GENERAL'S DEPARTMENT   This department was in charge of personnel, orders, and regulations. On June 16, 1775 an adjutant general had been authorized and on July 29, 1775 a deputy as well.[217] On May 18, 1776 there was also a deputy adjutant general in Virginia. On May 17, 1779 the department was to have 1 adjutant general, 2 assistants, and 1 clerk, plus deputies in the other field armies.[218] In 1782 the adjutant general was to have 1 deputy, 2 assistants, 1 clerk, and also a deputy and an assistant with the Southern Army.

CLOTHIER GENERAL'S DEPARTMENT   This department was

created in December, 1776 to procure clothing. It consisted of a clothier general with his various deputies, assistants, agents, and clerks.

ENGINEER'S DEPARTMENT   *See* Engineer's Department.

FIELD DEPARTMENT   The author is not certain just what this department was, but in 1782 it included 1 field commissary, 2 deputies, 5 conductors, and 2 clerks.

GEOGRAPHER'S DEPARTMENT   This was established in the latter part of the war for mapmaking. In 1782 it consisted of 2 geographers, 3 assistants, and some chain bearers.

HOSPITAL DEPARTMENT   In July, 1775 a director general and chief physician was appointed for the Continental Army. Little else was done above regimental level until May 18, 1776 when a hospital was authorized to be set up in Virginia of 1 director and chief physician, 2 surgeons, 1 apothecary, 6 surgeon's mates, 1 clerk, 1 storekeeper, 1 nurse for each 10 sick, and laborers as needed.[219] On April 8, 1777 three more hospitals were to be set up in the North, Middle, and Eastern states and the department was now to consist of 1 director general, 3 deputy director generals, 1 indeterminate assistant director general, 4 physician generals, 4 surgeon generals, and various surgeons, mates, nurses, and clerks to run the four hospitals.[220] In addition each field army was to have a physician and surgeon general. On September 30, 1780 the department was reorganized as 1 director of military hospitals, 3 assistant hospital physicians, 1 chief physician, 15 hospital physicians, 20 surgeon's mates, 1 purveyor, 1 assistant purveyor, 1 apothecary, 1 assistant apothecary, and clerks, stewards, nurses, and matrons for each hospital.[221] In the latter part of 1781 the Hospital Department was reorganized into the Medical Department (which see).

INSPECTOR GENERAL'S DEPARTMENT   This department was established in 1778 to check on the efficiency of the army. In August of that year the department was to have an inspector general with 4 infantry, 1 light infantry, and one cavalry sub-inspector. In 1782 the inspector general had 4 assistants and one clerk.

JUDGE ADVOCATE GENERAL'S DEPARTMENT   This department was in charge of administering military justice. On July 29, 1775 a judge advocate was appointed.[222] In 1782 the judge advocate had a deputy and another deputy was with the Southern Army.

MEDICAL DEPARTMENT   Resulting from a reorganization of the Hospital Department in late 1781, the Medical Department was to have 1 physician in chief and director of military hospitals, 12 surgeons, 24 surgeon's mates, 1 apothecary with 2 assistants, and 1 purveyor with 2 assistants.[223] On July 23, 1782 only the Southern Army was to have an assistant purveyor and an assistant apothecary, also the number of clerks and other personnel was reduced.[224]

COMMISSARY OF MILITARY STORES   By early 1776 this department had been established by both the Main and the Northern Armies. Military stores included all manner of arms and field equipment. In 1782 the department had 1 commissary, 2 deputies, 3 laboratory directors, 1 captain of artificers, 3 conductors, and 3 clerks. The department was closely linked with the Regiment of Artillery Artificers (which see).

COMMISSARY OF MUSTERS   June 16, 1775 a commissary of musters to keep correct account of unit rolls was authorized. Soon he was authorized a number of deputies.[225] The department gradually declined, most of its duties being taken over by the adjutant general or the inspector general.

PAYMASTER GENERAL'S DEPARTMENT   On June 16, 1775 a paymaster and deputy paymaster were authorized for the Continental Army and Separate Army respectively.[226] On January 9, 1776 two assistant paymasters were authorized for the Northern Army and on February 15, 1776 a deputy paymaster for the Virginia troops.[227] In 1782 the department consisted of the paymaster general, 2 deputies, and 3 assistant clerks.

PROVOST DEPARTMENT   Created in 1775. *See* Von Heer's Provost Troop.

QUARTERMASTER GENERAL'S DEPARTMENT   The quartermaster general's position was a very important one. He was overall coordinator of seeing that the troops in the field were supplied and looked after. His employees were numerous. On June 16, 1775 a quartermaster general for the Continental Army and a deputy quartermaster general for the Separate Army were appointed. Two assistant quartermasters and 40 clerks were soon added. On July 29, 1775 a wagonmaster and a master carpenter were to be appointed and by August there was an artificer company before Boston under Mr. Ayres. On January 9, 1776 a barrackmaster was appointed for the Northern Army. On March 28 a deputy quartermaster general was also added for the Southern Army and in July another for the Flying Camp. Finally on December 30, 1776 Congress boosted the Quartermaster Department of the Northern Army by authorizing artificers; a bateaux service of fifteen companies, each of a captain and 30 men; and four companies of carpenters, each of 1 captain and 25 men.[228] In 1777 Colonel Jedunathan Baldwin was authorized to raise companies of artificers for the Quartermaster Department of the Continental Army. By 1779 there were eleven companies of quartermaster artificers, mostly from Connecticut.[229] In November of that year congress ordered the artificers to be regimented and Washington planned to form them into ten companies the next February,[230] but this does not seem to have been done. In the reforms effective January 1, 1781 a regiment of eight companies each of 60 artificers was to be raised in Pennsylvania. The regiment was apparently to include both artillery artificers and quartermaster artificers, but it was never raised. Most of the remaining artificers were eventually sent to the Southern Department during 1781-82.[231]

By 1780 the Quartermaster General's Department was employing 3,000 men. In addition to the quartermaster artificers, there were subdepartments under the commissary general, wagonmaster general, and the overseer of boats, Each separate field army was to have a deputy quartermaster general, foragemaster general, and wagonmaster general.

The train of each army in 1780 was planned to include, in addition to a wagonmaster general and his deputy, 1 headquarters conductor, 1 staff conductor, and 1 conductor for each infantry brigade. Each member of a general's staff was allowed a 2-horsed cart; each general and field officer, a 4-horsed wagon; and each regimental staff and 80 marching men, a 4-horsed wagon.[232]

In 1782 the Quartermaster General's Department had declined to 1 quartermaster general, 1 deputy quartermaster general for the Southern Army, 8 state deputy quartermasters, 20 state assistant deputy quartermasters, 24 assistant deputy quartermasters with brigades in the field, 18 clerks and conductors, 1 commissary of forage, 2 assistant commissaries of forage, 1 deputy assistant commissary of forage with the Southern Army also with 2 assistants, 10 forage masters, 1 wagonmaster with his deputy with the Main Army, 1 deputy wagonmaster with his assistant for the Southern Army, 1 harbor master, 1 overseer of boats, and 4 captains, 1 captain lieutenant, 6 lieutenants, 20 sergeants, and 134 privates of artificers.

State Troops State troops may be defined as those troops who: 1) were raised at state initiative to defend that state or colony primarily 2) were paid and equipped by that state 3) were intended for full time service over a long period of time 4) looked to the state government for their orders. Unfortunately for the historian, very few so-called state troops comply with all four parts of this definition. Some state troops were sent out of their state for prolonged periods. Some were never paid by anyone. Some were not full-time troops. Some even served under Continental officers. There were, nevertheless, some troops who simply were not Continental troops and were not considered as militia either. Although this book is primarily concerned with Continental troops, a few words about these state troops seems in order as they often cooperated with the Continentals and are sometimes confused with them by writers. The brief state by state survey which follows is not intended as the last word on the state forces, but it is hoped it will be of value to the reader.

CONNECTICUT   Bradley's Battalion of Connecticut State Troops. May-December, 1776.

GEORGIA   In June, 1781 Jackson's Georgia Legion was raised to serve one year. It was to consist of 1 lieutenant colonel commandant, 1 major, 6 captains, 8 lieutenants, 1 sergeant major, 1 quartermaster sergeant, 1 saddler, 100 horsemen in three companies of dragoons, and 100 infantry in two companies. Each company was to have 3 noncommissioned officers and 1 musician. In January, 1782 the cavalry was cut to one troop of 40 privates. Disbanded August, 1782.

MARYLAND   In January, 1776 Smallwood's Regiment (which see), 7 independent infantry companies of 100 men each, 2 mattross companies, and 1 marine company were raised by the state. Smallwood's Regiment entered the Continental service that summer, the infantry companies that December. The mattrosses were reorganized as 3 companies during the autumn with men enlisted for the war. In June, 1777 it was provided that Continental companies could be organized from the men of the state mattrosses and in October, 1777 many of the mattrosses entered the Continental service under Captains Brown and Dorsey. In July, 1779 the remaining state mattrosses were sent to join the Main Army. In October, 1780 a 27 man cavalry troop and a 33 man infantry company were to be raised in Somerset and Worcester Counties by the state.

MASSACHUSETTS   In mid-1776 the state raised two infantry regiments and a train of artillery of seven companies to serve one year (later raised to three years). Coastguards were also raised. In July, 1777 two more regiments were raised to serve in Rhode Island. On

117

February 29, 1779 the artillery was cut to three companies and in April, 1780 to one.

NEW HAMPSHIRE   Information is fragmentary, but by the end of 1775 there were two companies of artillery and in August, 1776 there is mention of Gilman's State Regiment. Also various assorted rangers.

NEW JERSEY   On February 13, 1776 the East and West Artillery Companies were created. They were absorbed into the Continental service in 1777. In November, 1776 a brigade under Brigadier General Williamson of four battalions was enlisted for five months. The brigade is generally considered militia. On September 24, 1777 a new state artillery company was raised. On December 26, 1780, twelve companies of volunteer militia were called for one year to defend the frontiers and a smaller number for the same period on December 15, 1781.

NEW YORK   Hamilton's Artillery Company (and perhaps others) was raised in 1776 as a state unit. Various ranger companies served during the war.

NORTH CAROLINA   At various times between 1776-1779 there existed a state infantry regiment and a few troops of light horse. In 1781-82 there was a State Legionary Corps.

PENNSYLVANIA   In the spring of 1776 Atlee's State Battalion of Musketry, Miles' State Rifle Regiment of two battalions, and Proctor's State Artillery Company were raised and served through the year. In early 1777 there was a state artillery regiment and a state infantry regiment. The two regiments were taken into Continental service in July and November, 1777 respectively.

RHODE ISLAND   August 15, 1775 a regiment of 500 men was raised to defend the state for one year. Later a watch company was added. By the end of February, 1776 the state troops had been increased to two regiments, each of 750 men in twelve companies (one regiment also had an artillery company), who were to serve one year. During 1776 these two regiments were paid by Congress. December 10, 1776 state troops were to be a brigade of two infantry regiments, each of 750 men in eight companies, and one artillery regiment of 300 men in five companies, all to serve fifteen months. December 19, 1777 these men's service commitments were extended another fifteen months. On June 16, 1779 an infantry battalion of 930 men in nine companies, a light infantry battalion of four companies, and an artillery regiment were enlisted for one year. They mustered out in May, 1780.

SOUTH CAROLINA   In April, 1781 two regiments of regular light horse were to be raised by Colonel Henry Hampton and Colonel Middleton respectively. During the spring of 1782 Mayham's Legion was also a state unit.

VIRGINIA   From the summer of 1775 there were regimental-size bodies of state troops and minutemen. *(See* the 1st Virginia Regiment of 1775.) In 1776 various independent state troops of horse and foot were raised. They were discharged at year's end. Later state troops included the following corps. The 1st thru 3rd State Infantry Regiments were created in 1777 although only the 1st was fairly well organized, the 2nd and 3rd being pooled to form one battalion in January, 1778. Captain Decrome de la Porte and other officers of French descent were authorized to raise an independent corps in April, 1777 by the state. This French Company was in garrison at Williamsburg until August, 1778 when it seems to have been incorporated into the State Infantry Regiments. Marshall's State Artillery Regiment was raised in June, 1777 with a strength of ten companies. Marshall's Artillery Regiment served until 1781. Muter's Garrison Regiment consisting of eight companies was raised in June, 1778 to guard the harbor forts. Colonel Francis Taylor's Convention Guard Regiment was created in January, 1779 and actually raised in August of that year. This Convention Guard Regiment was probably the same as the Albemarle County Battalion (which see). Major John Nelson's State Cavalry Regiment was raised in May, 1779. It consisted of four troops, one of which was apparently detached to the Continental service in December while acting as prison guards.

The Western Regiments consisted of George Rogers Clarke's seven-company Illinois Regiment of 1779 and Crockett's Regiment of ten companies that served from early 1780 until sometime in 1782. John Rogers 35-man troop of Illinois Dragoons served alongside Clarke's Regiment during 1779-82 while a corps of Indian fighters under Major Slaughter was associated with Crockett's Regiment. In 1780 a detachment of the Garrison Regiment, Cavalry, and Artillery was sent south under Colonel Porterfield where it was cut to pieces at Camden. In 1781 the remnants of the 1st and 2nd State Infantry, the Cavalry, Artillery, and Garrison Regiment were all grouped under Lieutenant Colonel Charles Dabney.

On March 20, 1781 Alexander Spotswood was appointed brigadier general over two units to be raised by the state, but mobilized only in the case of invasion or threatened invasion of the state. The two legions commanded by Lieutenant Colonels John Taylor and

Everhard Mead respectively, were each to consist of six infantry companies and one cavalry troop, each company and troop having 100 men. During the turmoil of the year 1781, Spotswood's Legions were never called out, but the remnants of the old regular state regiments were present at Yorktown where they formed a provisional State Regiment. In January, 1782 the remnants of the old State Regiments were formed into Dabney's Virginia State Legion of three infantry companies, two troops of cavalry, and one small company of artillery. During 1782 Spotswood's Legions faded from existence, having never been properly mobilized. Dabney's State Legion of regulars continued to exist until it was disbanded by the state on April 24, 1783 after which time one troop of these state regulars was retained to guard the Virginia stores until late 1783 when they too were dismissed.

Captain John Steel's Independent Company   This Pennsylvania unit began as an independent company on January 13, 1777, but was later attached to Malcolm's Additional Continental Regiment. January 13, 1779 it was transferred into the new 11th Pennsylvania Regiment.

Stephenson's Maryland and Virginia Rifle Regiment   On June 17, 1776 Congress decided that the rifle companies from Maryland and Virginia serving in the Continental Army should be formed into a regiment. On June 27 Congress resolved that in addition to the three companies of riflemen from these states then serving at New York, there should be raised four more companies in Virginia, and two more in Maryland.[233] The men were to be enlisted for three years. Along with the German Battalion, this was the first Continental unit to be enlisted for over one year. Colonel Stephenson, the commander, was a Virginian. His second in command, Lieutenant Colonel Rawlings, was from Maryland. Recruitment of the regiment did not go well. Most of the regiment was captured at Fort Washington on November 16, 1776 and attempts to reorganize it as Rawlings' Additional Continental Regiment (which see) were not an outstanding success.

  COMMANDERS: Colonel Hugh Stephenson June 27, 1776-September, 1776.

         Lieutenant Colonel Moses Rawlings September-November 16, 1776.

Major Stevens' Independent Battalion of Continental Artillery   On November 9, 1776 Ebenezer Stevens, an officer of considerable experience in that arm, was appointed commander of the Continental artillery in the Northern Department. On February 11, 1778 Congress sanctioned the established fact that "the Corps of Artillery in the Northern Department...consist of three companies, distinct from Knox's Brigade."[234] In the fall of that year, however, it was decided that Stevens' Battalion should be made a part of the 3rd Battalion in Knox's Brigade and this was done.

Two Companies of Mohegan and Stockbridge Indians   In late 1776 it was proposed that two companies of Christian, partly Europeanized Stockbridge and Mohegan Indians be raised in the Northern Department. Congress disliked the plan and apparently very little further action was taken on it.[235]

Sunbury Artillery Company   *See* Captain Morris' Independent Artillery Company.

T

Colonel Thompson's Pennsylvania Rifle Regiment   *See* Pennsylvania
Rifle Regiment.

Colonel Thurston's Additional Continental Regiment   Colonel
Charles Thurston was commissioned to raise his regiment on
January 15, 1777. The regiment recruited in Virginia. The corps
merged with Gist's Ranger Corps on January 1, 1779.

V

Virginia Artillery Company   *See* 1st Battalion of Continental Artillery.

Virginia Light Dragoons   *See* 1st Regiment of Continental Light Dragoons, 3rd Regiment of Continental Light Dragoons, Lee's Legion.

1st Virginia Regiment of 1775   In June, 1775 the Virginia Convention ordered two regiments raised to defend Virginia. The regiments were to serve a maximum of one year. The 1st Virginia Regiment originally had eight companies, but in December it was raised to a strength of ten companies. After December 28 it was ordered reorganized for Continental service. February 13, 1776 the regiment was accepted for Continental service by Congress and the regiment served on till the end of 1776 when the switch to three year enlistments necessitated a major reorganization.[236]

    COMMANDERS: Colonel Patrick Henry July, 1775-February, 1776.

                      Colonel James Read February 13, 1776-December, 1776.

1st Virginia Regiment of 1777　　The 1st Virginia was reorganized in early 1777 and served until it was captured at Charleston on May 12, 1780.

COMMANDERS:　Colonel James Read January, 1777-September 29, 1777.
Colonel James Hendricks September 29, 1777-February 10, 1778.
Colonel Richard Parker February 10, 1778-April 24, 1780.
Lieutenant Colonel Burgess Ball April 24, 1780-February 12, 1781. After that date William Davies was colonel, although there never was a regiment for him to command, until 1783.

1st Virginia Battalion of 1781　　After the debacle at Charleston in May, 1780, Virginia made plans to field 5,000 drafted men in six battalions officered by what pitifully few Continental officers were in the state recruiting or on leave. In October a more definite plan to draft 3,000 militiamen into the Continental Army for eighteen months was adopted, but the enemy's invasion of the state doomed this plan to failure. Two temporary battalions, however, were recruited and served under Green and Hawes respectively at Guilford Courthouse. Later in the spring of 1781, Colonel Ferbinger was in charge of the Virginia Continentals—one battalion of mostly eighteen-month men. Ferbinger's battalion included a small band of music[237] and served at Yorktown. Ferbinger's battalion was merged into the ultimate 1st Virginia regiment on January 1, 1783. During 1782 Lieutenant Colonel Thomas Posey usually commanded the battalion.

1st Virginia Regiment of 1783　　On January 1, 1783 the remnants of Ferbinger's battalion from the Southern Army, the old 7th Virginia at Fort Pitt, and some new recruits at Winchester were pooled to make up the 1st Virginia Regiment or Battalion. The battalion was furloughed July 25, 1783.[238]

COMMANDER:　Colonel James Wood January 1, 1783-July 25, 1783.

2nd Virginia Regiment of 1775　　Created in June, 1775 by the Virginia Convention and intended to serve one year or less, the regiment originally had seven companies each of 68 privates. In

December it was raised to ten companies. After December 28, 1776 it was ordered reorganized for Continental service. On February 13, 1776 the regiment was accepted by Congress for Continental service and went on to serve until the end of 1776, when the change in enlistment policy resulted in major reorganization.

COMMANDERS: Colonel William Woodford June, 1775-September 3, 1776.

Lieutenant Colonel Alexander Spotswood September 3, 1776-February, 1777.

2nd Virginia Regiment of 1777   The 2nd Virginia Regiment was reorganized in early 1777 and served until it was captured at Charleston on May 12, 1780.

COMMANDERS: Colonel Alexander Spotswood February 21, 1777-October 9, 1777.

Colonel Christian Ferbinger September 26, 1777-January 1, 1783.

2nd Virginia Regiment of 1783   The 2nd Virginia Regiment or Battalion was formed on January 1, 1783 by appointing a major commandant and placing him over one company of 60 veterans drafted from the legionary corps and the artillery of the Southern Army and one company of 60 recruits. This small battalion was furloughed between June and August of 1783.[239]

COMMANDER: Major Smith Snead

3rd Virginia Regiment of 1776   In December, 1775 the Virginia government created this regiment of ten companies. On December 28, 1775 Congress asked for six battalions of Continentals from Virginia and this was one of them. Accepted by Congress on February 13, 1776, the regiment served through the year in the Continental Army. It underwent massive reorganization in early 1777.

COMMANDERS: Colonel Hugh Mercer February 13, 1776-June 6, 1776.

Colonel George Weedon August 13, 1776-February 21, 1777. Weedon was the lieutenant colonel until August 13.

3rd Virginia Regiment of 1777   The 3rd Virginia Regiment was reorganized in early 1777 and served until it was captured at Charleston on May 12, 1780.

COMMANDERS: Colonel Thomas Marshall February 21, 1777-December 4, 1777. Lieutenant Colonel William Heth December 4, 1777-May 2, 1780. Heth was made colonel on April 30, 1778. Colonel Abraham Buford commanded a paper 3rd Regiment from February 12, 1781 to January 1, 1783.

4th Virginia Regiment of 1776 This regiment had an organizational history identical to the 3rd Virginia Regiment of 1776 (which see).
COMMANDERS: Colonel Adam Stephen February 13, 1776-September 4, 1776.
Colonel Thomas Elliot September 3, 1776-December, 1776.

4th Virginia Regiment of 1777 The 4th Virginia was reorganized in early 1777. On about May 10, 1779 it seems that the remaining enlisted men of the regiment were incorporated into the 3rd Virginia and on May 12, 1780 the regiment's officers were captured at Charleston.
COMMANDERS: Colonel Thomas Elliot January, 1777-September 28, 1777.
Colonel Robert Lawson April 1, 1777-December 17, 1777.
Colonel John Neville September 14, 1778-January 1, 1783. Neville was actually captured at Charleston.

5th Virginia Regiment of 1776 This regiment had an organizational history identical to the 3rd Virginia Regiment of 1776 (which see).
COMMANDERS: Colonel William Peachey February 13, 1776-May 7, 1776.
Colonel Charles Scott May 7, 1776-December, 1776.

5th Virginia Regiment of 1777 The 5th Regiment was reorganized early in 1777 and served until September 14, 1778 when it was incorporated into the 3rd Virginia Regiment.
COMMANDERS: Colonel Charles Scott January, 1777-April 1, 1777.
Colonel Josiah Parker April 1, 1777-July 12, 1778.
Colonel Abraham Buford May 16, 1778-September 14, 1778.

5th Virginia Regiment of 1778   Until September 14, 1778 this had been the 7th Virginia Regiment. The regiment had its enlisted men pooled into either the 1st or 2nd Virginia Detachment, this occurring probably early in 1780. Both they and their officers were captured at Charleston on May 12, 1780.

COMMANDER: Colonel William Russel September 14, 1778-January 1, 1783. Russel was captured at Charleston.

6th Virginia Regiment of 1776   This regiment had an organizational history identical to the 3rd Virginia Regiment (which see).

COMMANDER: Colonel Mordecai Buckner February 13, 1776-January 23, 1777.

6th Virginia Regiment of 1777   The 6th Virginia was reorganized early in 1777 and served until September 14, 1778 when it was incorporated into the 2nd Virginia Regiment.

COMMANDERS: Lieutenant Colonel James Hendricks January 23, 1777-September 29, 1777.
Colonel John Gibson October 27, 1777-September 14, 1778.

6th Virginia Regiment of 1778   Prior to the reorganization of September 14, 1778 this had been the 10th Virginia. The regiment's enlisted men were pooled into either the 1st or 2nd Virginia, probably early in 1780, and together with their officers were captured at Charleston on May 12, 1780.

COMMANDER: Colonel John Green September 14, 1778-January 1, 1783.

7th Virginia Regiment of 1776   The 7th Virginia Regiment was created in December, 1775 by the Virginia government. It had ten companies. On March 25, 1776 Congress voted to take the regiment into Continental service. At the end of the year, the change in enlistment policy necessitated major reorganization in this as well as the other Virginia regiments.

COMMANDERS: Colonel William Dangerfield February 29, 1776-August 13, 1776.
Colonel William Crawford August 14, 1776-March 4, 1777.

7th Virginia Regiment of 1777   The regiment was reorganized early

127

in 1777. On September 14, 1778 it was redesignated the 5th Virginia Regiment.

COMMANDER: Colonel Alexander McClanachan October 7, 1776-May 13, 1778.
Lieutenant Colonel Holt Richeson May 13, 1778-September 14, 1778.

7th Virginia Regiment of 1778   Formerly designated the 11th Virginia Regiment prior to September 14, 1778. Around early 1780 its enlisted men were pooled into either the 1st or 2nd Virginia Detachment and together with their officers were captured at Charleston on May 12, 1780.

COMMANDER: Colonel Daniel Morgan September 14, 1778-June, 1779.
Major Thomas Posey June, 1779-February, 1780.
Lieutenant Colonel Samuel Cabell February, 1780-May 12, 1780 when he was captured.

7th Virginia Regiment of 1781   Unlike the other Virginia regiments of February 12, 1781 reorganization, this regiment actually existed. It was the former 9th Virginia under Colonel Gibson. The regiment merged into the 1st Virginia on January 1, 1783.

8th Virginia Regiment of 1776   The 8th Virginia Regiment had an organizational history identical to the 7th Virginia of 1776 (which see). This was the first Virginia regiment to serve outside the state, seeing action at Charleston in June, 1776 and later doing duty briefly at Savannah. The regiment consisted largely of German settlers in the Shenandoah Valley, but one company came from the Fort Pitt area.[240]

COMMANDER: Colonel Peter Muhlenberg March 1, 1776-February 21, 1777.

8th Virginia Regiment of 1777   The regiment was reorganized in early 1777 and served until September 14, 1778 when it was incorporated into the 4th Virginia Regiment.

COMMANDERS: Colonel Abraham Bowman January 30, 1777-October, 1777.
Colonel William Nelson October 15, 1777-December, 1777.
Colonel John Neville December 11, 1777-September 14, 1778.

8th Virginia Regiment of 1778   Formerly designated the 12th Virginia Regiment prior to September 14, 1778. Around early 1780 its enlisted men were pooled into either the 1st or 2nd Virginia Detachment and together with their officers were captured at Charleston on May 12, 1780.

COMMANDER: Colonel James Wood September 14, 1778-January 1, 1783.

9th Virginia Regiment of 1776   The 9th Virginia Regiment had an organizational history almost identical to the 7th Virginia Regiment of 1776 (which see). However, as the regiment was originally intended to guard the East Shore of Virginia, it had only five companies although it was later raised to seven and ultimately to ten companies.

COMMANDERS: Colonel Thomas Fleming March 2, 1776-August, 1776.
Lieutenant Colonel George Matthews August, 1776-February, 1777.

9th Virginia Regiment of 1777   The 9th Virginia Regiment was reorganized in early 1777. Practically all of it was captured at Germantown on October 4, 1777 and the 1st Virginia State Regiment was sent to take its place temporarily.

COMMANDER: Colonel George Matthews February 10, 1777-captured October 4, 1777.

9th Virginia Regiment of 1778   Prior to September 14, 1778 this was the 13th Virginia Regiment. During 1779 and 1780 this regiment was on garrison duty at the frontier and thus was the only regiment of the Virginia Line to escape the disaster at Charleston. In February, 1781 the men of this regiment were transferred to the 7th Virginia Regiment in the paper reorganization of the Virginia Continentals. On January 1, 1783 these men were transferred to the 1st Virginia Regiment (which see).

COMMANDER: Colonel John Gibson September 14, 1778-February 12, 1781.

10th Virginia Regiment of 1777   The 10th Virginia Regiment was created in October, 1776 to help fill Virginia's expanded quota of troops. The colonel was commissioned on November 12. On September 14, 1778 the regiment was redesignated as the 6th Virginia Regiment.

10th Virginia Regiment of 1778

COMMANDERS: Colonel Edward Stevens November 12, 1776-January 31, 1778.
Colonel John Green January 26, 1778-September 14, 1778.

10th Virginia Regiment of 1778   Formerly designated the 14th Virginia Regiment prior to September 14, 1778. Around early 1780 its enlisted men were pooled into either the 1st or 2nd Virginia Detachment and together with their officers were captured at Charleston on May 12, 1780.

COMMANDER: Colonel William Davies September 14, 1778-February 12, 1781.

11th Virginia Regiment of 1777   This regiment had an organizational history very similar to the 10th Virginia Regiment of 1777 (which see). Recruits for this regiment and the 15th were largely gathered by Daniel Morgan. The recruits for the 11th Regiment included five companies that had originally been intended for the Maryland and Virginia Rifle Regiment (which see).[241]. On September 14, 1778 this regiment was redesignated the 7th Virginia Regiment.

COMMANDER: Colonel Daniel Morgan November 12, 1776-September 14, 1778.

11th Virginia Regiment of 1778   Formerly designated the 15th Virginia Regiment prior to September 14, 1778. Around early 1780 its enlisted men were pooled into either the 1st or 2nd Virginia Detachment and together with their officers were captured at Charleston on May 12, 1780. Some early histories state that the 11th Virginia was the regiment cut to pieces by Tarleton at the Waxhaws on May 29, 1780, but this is an error. The commanding officer of the Continentals at the Waxhaws was the colonel of the 11th Virginia, but his men were actually new recruits or recalled veterans intended for the various regiments of the Virginia Line.

COMMANDER: Colonel Abraham Buford September 14, 1778-February 12, 1781.

12th Virginia Regiment   This regiment had an organizational history almost identical with the 10th Virginia Regiment of 1777 (which see). On September 14, 1778 it was redesignated the 8th Virginia Regiment.

COMMANDER: Colonel James Wood November 12, 1776-September 14, 1778.

130

13th Virginia Regiment   This regiment had an organizational history almost identical with the 10th Virginia Regiment of 1777 (which see). On September 14, 1778 it was redesignated the 9th Virginia Regiment.

COMMANDER: Colonel William Russel November 19, 1776-September 14, 1778.

14th Virginia Regiment   This regiment had an organizational history almost identical with the 10th Virginia Regiment of 1777 (which see). On September 14, 1778 it was redesignated the new 10th Virginia Regiment.

COMMANDERS: Colonel Charles Lewis November 12, 1776-March 28, 1778.
Colonel William Davies March 20, 1778-September 14, 1778.

15th Virginia Regiment   This regiment had an organizational history almost identical with the 10th Virginia Regiment of 1777 (which see). On September 14, 1778 it was redesignated the 11th Virginia Regiment.

COMMANDERS: Colonel David Mason November 12, 1776-July 1, 1777.
Lieutenant Colonel James Innis 1777.
Lieutenant Colonel Gustavus B. Wallace March 20, 1778-September 14, 1778.

Virginia Detachments   Apparently early in the year 1780, if not sooner, the enlisted men of the depleted 5th, 6th, 7th, 8th, 10th, and 11th Virginia Regiments were gathered together and formed into two temporary detachments of battalion size. The officers of the 4th through 8th and the 10th and 11th Virginia Regiments took turns commanding them. The two detachments and all the officers were subsequently captured at Charleston on May 12, 1780. The 1st and 2nd Virginia Detachments seem to have considerable precedent in Virginia. Virginia had an elaborate recruiting system which utilized militia officers to gather recruits to send to the Continental Army and in times of emergency it appears that temporary, but numbered, units were formed from the available companies of Continental recruits for the Continental regiments and from companies of militia.

Virginia Rifle Companies

Virginia Rifle Companies   June 14, 1775 the Continental Congress called on Virginia to raise two rifle companies to serve Congress until the end of the year. Each company was to have 1 captain, 3 lieutenants, 4 sergeants, 4 corporals, 1 drummer or trumpeter, and 68 privates. These companies were very promptly raised and marched to join the Continental Army at Boston. Some of the men were later detached for Arnold's Canadian expedition. Most of the rest apparently went home when their enlistments expired at the end of the year. Those that stayed with the army were probably eventually absorbed into Stephenson's Maryland and Virginia Rifle Regiment (which see) in mid-1776.

COMMANDERS: Captain Daniel Morgan
OF
COMPANIES   Captain Hugh Stephenson

Virginia State Regiments   Between 1777 and 1779 Virginia apparently retained three regiments of infantry. These units were not under the direction of Congress, but were strictly the Army of the State of Virginia. The small numbers of the Continentals from Virginia in 1778-1779, however, led Virginia to send the 1st and 2nd Regiments of the Virginia State Line to serve along with the Virginia Continentals where they remained until the end of the 1779 campaign. The 1st Regiment was commanded by Colonel George Gibson. In 1781 a Virginia State Regiment or Legion served in the Yorktown campaign alongside the Virginia militia. *See* State Troops, Virginia.

Virginia State Troops Guarding the Convention Prisoners   The Virginia infantry battalion and troop of light horse guarding the prisoners from Saratoga were to be considered Continental troops while guarding the prisoners, according to Congressional action of December 10, 1779. The infantry may be the Albemarle County Battalion (which see).[242]

Captain Von Heer's Provost Troop of Light Dragoons   Although there was a provost in 1775 and men had been assigned to assist him as early as 1776, not until May and June of 1778 was a permanent provost company formed. This 1778 force was mounted and equipped as a light dragoon troop of 1 captain, 4 lieutenants, 1 clerk, 1 quartermaster's sergeant, 2 sergeants, 5 corporals, 2 trumpeters, 4 excarabineers (executioners) and 43 privates. The men were drafted from the various brigades of the army. The provosts, Provost Corps, or Marchesie Corps as it was sometimes called, was intended to maintain order in the rear of the Main Army, picking up deserters and skulkers. The troop also performed some of the other duties of modern military police. By July 9, 1781 the Provosts had been placed on Pennsylvania's quota and this was none too soon for Washington stated the corps' enlistments were about up.[243] In February, 1782 Von Heer was recruiting new men and on April 25, 1782 thirty provosts were with the Main Army.[244] In September, 1782 the Provost Corps was attached to Washington's Life Guard, but not incorporated into it. Captain Von Heer had, prior to his appointment as provost in 1778, served as an officer in Armand's Corps and he brought many foreigners into the troop with him. Von Heer although not an American native, seems to have been a good officer and was promoted to the rank of major before he was discharged. Sometime between May 26 and September, 1783 the provosts were furloughed, but General Washington persuaded a sergeant, a corporal, and eight provosts to stay with him until October 3, 1783 to carry his dispatches.[245] Some of these men may have stayed until November, but at any rate they were among the last horsemen in the Continental Army.

W

Wagoners   *See* Staff Departments, Quartermaster Department.

Colonel Ward's Connecticut Regiment   Ward's Regiment seems to have actually been the additional Continental battalion from New Hampshire authorized by Congress May 14, 1776. The regiment was to serve until May 14, 1777. The unit was actually made up of Connecticut men. The regiment joined Washington's army and participated in the New York campaign, the subsequent retreat, and the victory at Trenton. In May, 1777 the regiment disbanded as scheduled.[246]

Colonel Warner's Continental Regiment   On June 23, 1775 Congress recommended that "Green Mountain Boys" from the backwoods of New York be recruited for the Separate Army under Schuyler. Accordingly Seth Warner's Battalion was created as 1 lieutenant colonel, 1 major, and 500 men in seven companies, each company officered by 1 captain and 2 lieutenants. The battalion served in Canada in the winter of 1775-1776 where it was pretty well cut to pieces. On July 5, 1776 Congress promoted Warner to colonel and authorized him to take such officers as had returned from Canada and reraise his corps, its enlistments having largely expired months before.[247] Warner's Regiment was retained by Congress for several years. Some modern writers list it as one of the sixteen additional regiments, yet it seems more likely that like the two Canadian regiments, this regiment was considered neither as a part of any state's Continental quota nor an additional regiment, but rather a special unit apart. Warner's Regiment served in the Saratoga campaign of 1777 and subsequently on garrison duty at Fort Anne and Fort George. It was disbanded by General Order effective January 1, 1781.

General Washington's Life Guard   The Life Guard was formed on March 12, 1776 to safeguard the general's person and baggage. It was an infantry company officered by a captain and a lieutenant. The men were to be between 5'8" and 5'10" tall. The Guard was disbanded around February 10, 1777, but May 1, 1777 it was again organized as 1 captain, 1 lieutenant, 4 sergeants, 4 corporals, 1 drummer, 1 fifer, and 47 privates. The men were to be 5'9" to 5'10" tall and only "Americans born" could serve in the Guard. On March 1, 1778 the Life Guard was ordered cut to 40 rank and file who were mostly Virginians, but on March 19 men were detached from all the regiments of the Main Army to serve in the corps. The reorganized Life Guard had 1 captain, 3 lieutenants, 1 surgeon, 4 sergeants, 3 corporals, 2 drummers, 1 fifer, and 136 privates. The Life Guard was used by Von Steuben as a demonstration model to give instructions in drill and he soon developed the Life Guard into the best drilled organization in the entire army. The Guard served through the war. On June 6, 1783 it was furloughed. At that time it consisted in addition to commissioned officers, of 4 sergeants, 3 corporals, 1 drum major, 2 drummers, 2 fifers, and 52 privates. After the Life Guard was furloughed, various ordinary guard duty details assumed its protection function. Ten days later, on June 16, 1783, a New Hampshire detail of 38 men, including 12 mounted, assumed that duty until November or December.

In addition to the infantry of the Life Guard, cavalry details were often assigned to escort the general and carry his dispatches. These troopers were dubbed the "cavalry of the Life Guard". From May 1, 1777 until September 26, 1778 this detachment was from the 3rd Light Dragoons, but afterwards these detachments were taken from the other dragoon regiments or from Von Heer's Provost Troop.[248]

COMMANDERS: From March 13, 1776 Captain Caleb Gibbs commanded the Guard. Gibbs was made a major July 29, 1778. On January 1, 1783 Gibbs was replaced by Lieutenant William Colfax. Colfax was made a captain on April 1, 1783. Lieutenant Bezaleel Howe replaced Colfax on September 5, 1783.

Lieutenant Colonel William Washington's Light Dragoons   *See* the 3rd Regiment of Continental Light Dragoons.

Wayne's Light Infantry   During the 1779 campaign the Light Infantry Corps of the Main Army was under the command of Brigadier General Anthony Wayne. The command consisted of four provisional regiments each of about 400 men. Internal organization of two of the regiments is mentioned. They are:

Colonel Ferbinger's Regiment made up of the 1st Battalion under Lieutenant Colonel Fleury (a French volunteer) with 1 Virginia company, 2 Pennsylvania companies, 1 Maryland company; and the 2nd Battalion under Major Posey with 4 Virginia companies.
Connecticut Regiment of 1st and 2nd Battalions each with 4 companies of Connecticut light infantry.

Captain Jacob Weaver's Independent Company   Annexed to the 10th Pennsylvania Regiment on November 7, 1777.

Colonel Samuel B. Webb's Additional Continental Regiment   Webb's Regiment was created January 1, 1777. It was raised mostly in Connecticut and was perhaps the most successful of all the additional regiments. Somehow Webb's Regiment was always in uniform—they wore scarlet coats and the regiment seems to have been well trained and effective in battle. It even had a band. In mid-May, 1780, Connecticut moved to take the regiment into its quota and this was approved by Congress on June 23. The regiment was numbered the 9th Connecticut on July 18, 1780. *See* 9th Connecticut Regiment.

Western Department   The Western Department was organized in 1778 around Fort Pitt to secure the frontiers of western New York, Pennsylvania, and Virginia.

Captain Wilkie's Independent Company   This Pennsylvania unit was incorporated into the 11th Pennsylvania Regiment on January 13, 1779, having formerly been attached to Malcolm's Additional Continental Regiment.

Captain James Willing's Independent Marine Company   The exact status of this company is somewhat hazy. One wonders if it should be considered as army or navy or even as a private military company. It is listed as consisting of 1 captain, 2 lieutenants, a carpenter, a coxswain, 3 sergeants, 2 corporals, and 24 privates. These men served aboard the boat *"Rattletrap"* operating against the British on the Mississippi River between January 10, 1778 and June 3, 1779. Many of these men subsequently entered the Virginia state service in the Illinois country.

Captain Woolverton's Independent Company   This company was accepted for service by Congress on March 19, 1776. Its pay was to commence when it drew arms. No further information.[249]

Wooster's Provisional Regiment   This regiment was formed in Canada in January, 1776 from those men of the old 1st, 4th, and 5th Connecticut Regiments who chose to remain in Canada after their enlistments expired at the end of 1775. This temporary regiment broke up about May, 1776.

Y

Captain Young's Artillery Company   This company was raised in Georgia about mid-1777. On February 19, 1778 Captain Lee's Artillery Company was incorporated into it.[250] No further information.

Brief Organizational History
of the Continental Army

It is difficult to pick one date and call it the day the Continental Army was created. Should one say it was April 19, 1775 when the first militia mustered on Lexington green? Or, should one say the date was May 25, 1775, when Congress authorized its first payment for soldiers to be recruited in New York? Was the date June 14 when Congress voted to take the four New England armies around Boston into its pay and passed its first resolution that actually called for troops to be raised? Was it June 16 when an overall commander was appointed for all troops in the pay of the Continental Congress? Probably it it safest to say that the Continental Army evolved gradually between April and June of 1775. Its original purpose was defensive as it was intended primarily to prevent retribution against the rebellious colonies by forces of the British government. Over the next twelve months this army gradually became the prime military element in the struggle for the independence of the thirteen colonies.

Enlistments during the first year of the war were almost exclusively for six months or until the end of the year. About the only exception to this was in some of the southern states where the term of enlistment was worded ambiguously without mentioning any specific time period. Even the troops specifically called for by Congress were to be enlisted only to the end of the year. The short enlistments were in the militia tradition of the colonists and few people expected the difficulties with the British government would last more than a few months anyway.

The year dragged on, however, with no resolution of the political differences with Britain and in October it became increasingly clear that an

army would be needed for a longer period than had been originally antici-
pated. Accordingly on November 4, 1775 it was decided that future enlistments should be for one year and that the army around Boston should be
completely reorganized on January 1, 1776. The New England states and
Pennsylvania were accordingly each assigned a quota of battalions of one-
year men to recruit for this force.

The War grew in scale through 1776 and by September of that year it
was obvious that it would be a long struggle. It was then decided to reorganize the Continental Army as a formation enlisted for the duration of
the war. New troop quotas were assigned each of the thirteen states. This
resolution had been foreshadowed by the June 27 resolution that called for
the Maryland and Virginia Rifle Regiment and the German Battalion to
be enlisted for three years.

On November 12, 1776 the September resolution was softened somewhat to allow men to enlist for either three years or for the War, at their
option. Many legislators resisted the idea of long term enlistments. These
men usually preferred a system of rotating the militia in and out of active
service so that all men served for a short period of time. They feared a
standing army as a threat to civil liberty. Their opponents, on the other
hand, pointed out the deficiencies of the militia in equipment and discipline. Each faction claimed the other's plan was more expensive.

In hindsight, it appears the plan to rotate the militia on and off active
duty was impractical owing to the communication system of the day and
the difficulty in providing it with essential discipline. Most historians are
quick to see this and dismiss the faction against a long service army as
idealistic fools. These historians fail to see the well founded fear of the
anti-army legislators, the fear of a military seizure of political power.

Over the winter of 1776-1777 the Continental Army was reorganized
again, this time on the basis of three-year and "duration of the War"
enlistments. In this reorganization for long term service three major short-
comings in the organization of the Army soon came to stand out.

First, Congress—in its enthusiasm and later in its panic—authorized
more units than could reasonably have been expected to reach effective
strength. Congress, with control of a population only a third of that of
Great Britain, had authorized an Army almost as large as the whole British
Army. The September legislation may be excused as an overestimate of
strength, but the December "Addition" bears the mark of panic legislation. This December 27, 1776 legislation gave Washington the power to
raise at his own initiative thousands of dragoons, artillerists, and artificers,
and also sixteen additional infantry regiments. Washington reluctantly attempted to raise most of the units allowed by the Addition, hoping the
more recruiters he had out the more recruits they would bring in. Actually

the Addition proved to be a great mistake because the states had no responsibility for providing the additional regiments with men and equipment and any support the states gave the additional regiments was not credited toward fulfilling the quotas required of them by Congress, quotas they had trouble enough fulfilling as it was. Slipshod legislation reflecting wild enthusiasm and panic rather than realistic evaluation of danger and the resources to meet it would continue to plague American military legislation for many years to come.

Secondly, all European armies had regimental depots of some sort to assemble, train, and equip recruits in a systematic matter. In the Continental Army the regimental depot was largely unknown and supply and recruitment were carried out in the most primitive and haphazard manner. Only in Virginia and possibly Connecticut does there seem to have been any attempt at systematic recruitment. It is true the 18th Century regimental depots were not the complex centers they were to become in the next century and that the British Army was always among the most backward in its depot organization, but the absolute neglect of depots in America seems almost incredible. This contempt for organized recruiting and training of replacements would plague the Continental Army and the later United States Army most seriously through the years.

The final defect in the Continental Army was shared to some extent by other armies of the day and even today is sometimes observed. This was the presence of numerous independent corps of various size. These units were usually commanded by junior officers. These officers quite often refused to take orders from their immediate superiors in nominal rank, saying they took orders from the commander of the Army only. Often this resulted in a needless fragmentation of manpower and other resources.

As the War continued various expedients were tried to boost the manpower of the Army. It was planned to draft militiamen into the Continental Army for short terms, but this was not done to any extent. By legislative action of March 13-15, 1779 the light dragoons, artillery, artificers, and independent corps were counted in the quotas of the states where they were enlisted and finally on January 31, 1780 all men in the Continental Army were to be counted on the quotas of the states where they were enlisted. The overall quotas of men required from the various states was reduced at this time in hopes that the more realistic quotas would encourage recruiting. Plans were formulated to form infantry battalions with Negro privates and white officers and sergeants in South Carolina, but this was not done, although Negro privates were numerous in the ranks of the infantry from North Carolina and further north.

The year of 1780 was perhaps the blackest year in the history of the Continental Army. Early in the year many of the men who had signed up for three years early in 1777 were discharged. Then came the staggering losses of Charleston and Camden which all but demolished the infantry organizations of half the states.

In October and November of 1780 a new organizational plan was drawn up for the Continental Army. This plan went into effect January 1, 1781 and provided the soundest basis for organization the Continental Army ever had—even a tiny regimental depot was at last created in the infantry regiments. Unfortunately, due to the disruptive presence of the enemy in the southern states much of the 1781 reorganization plan was impossible to carry out. The southern Continentals finished the war in provisional units created when and where possible, many of them even being drafted or enlisted for 18 months.

After the victory at Yorktown there was a general decline in American interest in military operations. The war had been long and the people of the states and their representatives in government were tired. Many of the Continental soldiers were exhausted. When preliminary peace was signed in November, 1782 the situation in America grew very strained. In early 1783 near chaos struck the Southern Army. Half of William Washington's dragoons simply mounted up and set off for home, claiming the War was now over. In the Main Army there were also disturbances, and rumblings of a military coup were heard. It is a tribute to most of the soldiers that the disturbances were not worse, but they were serious.

The Continental Army was gradually reduced in the early months of 1783 and after June 12, 1783 all men who had been enlisted to serve for the War were granted furloughs as were just about all the recruits from the states south of New England. The New England recruits were retained to watch the British in New York until November 5, 1783 when all but 1,000 men were discharged, the furloughed veterans having already been discharged a few days before. On November 15 the Southern Army was likewise disbanded so that after November 25, 1783, there were only the 1,000 soldiers at New York in a country now at peace. On June 2, 1784 this force was ordered reduced to 80 privates and a few officers who were to guard the military stores at West Point and Fort Pitt. These 80 men were later absorbed into what became the United States Army.

The Size of the Continental Army

The author has unfortunately been unable to find enough information to make reliable estimates of the size of the entire Continental Army at any one time. General Knox as Secretary of War in Washington's first presidential administration compiled a report on this matter to Congress. Knox admitted his report contained inaccuracies; some troops not being counted while others must have been counted twice. Still Knox's figures appear to be about all we have to go on. For the years of the War he gives the number of Continental regular troops as follows:

1775	27,443
1776	46,891
1777	34,820
1778	32,899
1779	27,699
1780	21,015
1781	13,292
1782	14,256
1783	13,476

Tending to support these figures is an actual letter of General Washington's of January, 1780 which states that the returns of the entire Army except for the South Carolina and Georgia contingents indicated there were 27,099 men including 14,998 who were enlisted for the duration of the War.

Based on figures later released by the British government, the author estimates that the following numbers of British, Loyalist, and German troops were present in the American theatre of operations (including Canada, Florida, and the West Indies) during the war years.

June, 1777 28,000
March, 1778 33,750
August, 1778 34,000
November, 1778 22,550
February, 1779 26,750
May, 1779 25,600
December, 1779 29,600
May, 1780 31,600
August, 1780 35,000
December, 1780 38,200
September, 1781 36,600
November 1, 1781 29,400

By 1780 the British Army numbered over 80,000 men at home and abroad.

Continental Army Brigades and Their Compositions

Much reference is made to various brigades of the Continental Army, therefore these notes on the composition of some of them at various times may be of interest.

Poor's Brigade on September 12, 1777
    1st New Hampshire Regiment
    2nd New Hampshire Regiment
    3rd New Hampshire Regiment

Learned's Brigade on September 12, 1777
    2nd Massachusetts Regiment
    8th Massachusetts Regiment
    9th Massachusetts Regiment
    1st Canadian Regiment (?)

Varnum's Brigade on October 16, 1777
    1st Rhode Island Regiment
    2nd Rhode Island Regiment
    4th Connecticut Regiment
    8th Connecticut Regiment

Huntington's Brigade on October 16, 1777
    1st Connecticut Regiment
    5th Connecticut Regiment
    7th Connecticut Regiment

Troops Wintering at Valley Forge, Pa. 1777—1778

Parson's 1st Connecticut Brigade Fall, 1778 to January 1, 1781
3rd Connecticut Regiment
4th Connecticut Regiment
6th Connecticut Regiment
8th Connecticut Regiment

Huntington's 2nd Connecticut Brigade Fall, 1778 to January 1, 1781
1st Connecticut Regiment
2nd Connecticut Regiment
5th Connecticut Regiment
7th Connecticut Regiment

Smallwood's 1st Maryland Brigade on September 13, 1779
1st Maryland Regiment
3rd Maryland Regiment
5th Maryland Regiment
7th Maryland Regiment
2nd Maryland Brigade on October 27, 1779
4th Maryland Regiment
6th Maryland Regiment

Huntington's Brigade from January, 1783-June, 1783
1st Connecticut Regiment
2nd Connecticut Regiment
3rd Connecticut Regiment

TROOPS WINTERING AT
VALLEY FORGE, PA.
1777-1778

List of General and Field Officers who belonged to Brigades and Regiments as arranged and encamped at Valley Forge, Pennsylvania, in the winter and spring of 1777 and 1778.

REGIMENT	COLONEL	LIEUT. COLONEL	MAJOR
Brig. Gen. William Woodford's Brigade			
7th Va.	A. McClanachan	Holt Richardson	John Webb
11th Va.	Daniel Morgan	John Cropper	Thomas Snead
Brig. Gen. Charles Scott's Brigade			
8th Va.	Abraham Bowman	John Markham	Alexander Morgan
12th Va.	James Wood	John Neville	George Slaughter
Continental	Wm. Grayson	Levin Powell	John Thornton

Troops Wintering at Valley Forge, Pa. 1777—1778

Brig. Gen. Anthony Wayne's Brigade

1st Pa.	James Chambers	Thomas Robinson	James Moore
2d Pa.	Henry Bicker	Henry Miller	Wm. Williams
7th Pa.	Wm. Irwin	David Grier	Samuel Hay
10th Pa.	George Nagel	Adam Hubley	James Grier

Second Pennsylvania Brigade

4th Pa.	Lambert Cadwalader	Wm. Butler	Thomas Church
5th Pa.	Francis Johnston	Persifer Frazer	James Taylor
8th Pa.	Daniel Broadhead	Stephen Bayard	Frederick Vernon
11th Pa.	Richard Humpton	Caleb North	Francis Mentges

Brig. Gen. Enoch Poor's Brigade

3d N.H.	Alexander Scammell	Henry Dearborn	James Norris
1st N.H.	Joseph Cilley	George Reid	Wm. Scott
2d N.H.	Nathan Hale	Jeremiah Gilman	Benjamin Titcomb
2d N.Y.	Philip Van Cortland	Fred'k. Weisenfels	Nicholas Fish
4th N.Y.	Henry B. Livingston	Pierre R. de Roussi	Benjamin Ledyard

Brig. Gen. John Glover's Brigade

4th Mass.	William Shepard	Ebenezer Sprout	Warham Parks
1st Mass.	Joseph Vose	Elijah Vose	Thomas Cogswell
13th Mass.	Edward Wigglesworth	Dudley Coleman	John Porter
15th Mass.	Timothy Bigelow	Henry Haskell	Hugh Maxwell

Brig. Gen. Ebenezer Learned's Brigade

2d Mass.	John Bailey	Ezra Badlam	Andrew Peters
9th Mass.	James Wesson	James Mellen	
8th Mass.	Michael Jackson	John Brooks	William Hull

Brig. Gen. John Paterson's Brigade

10th Mass.	Thomas Marshall	Joseph Thompson	Nathaniel Winslow
14th Mass.	Gamaliel Bradford	Barakieh Bassett	Samuel Tubbs
11th Mass.	Benjamin Tupper	Noah M. Littlefield	Wm. Lithgow
12th Mass.	Samuel Brewer	Samuel Carlton	Tobias Fernald

Brig. Gen. George Weedon's Brigade

2d Va.	Christian Febiger	Richard Parker	Ralph Faulkner
4th Va.	Isaac Read	Thomas Gaskins	Issac Beall
10th Va.	John Green	Lewis Willis	Samuel Hawes
3d Va.	Thomas Marshall	William Heth	John Hays
14th Va.	Charles Lewis		George Stubblefield and S.J. Cabell

Brig. Gen. Peter Muhlenberg's Brigade

1st Va.	James Hendricks	Robert Ballard	Edmund B. Dickinson
5th Va.	Josiah Parker	Abraham Buford	Thomas Gaskins
9th Va.	George Matthews	Burgess Ball	John Fitzgerald
6th Va.	John Gibson	Charles Simms	Samuel Hopkins
13th Va.	Wm. Russell	Richard Campbell	Richard Taylor
German Regt.		Ludowick Weltner	Daniel Burchardt

Troops Wintering at Valley Forge, Pa. 1777—1778

Brig. Gen. William Maxwell's Brigade

1st N.J.	Matthias Ogden	David Brearley	Joseph Morris
2d N.J.	Israel Shreve	Wm. De Hart	Daniel Piatt and Richard Howell
3d N.J.	Elias Dayton	Francis Barber	Joseph Bloomfield
4th N.J.	Ephraim Martin	David Rhea	John Conway

Brig. Gen. Thomas Conway's Brigade

3d Pa.	Thomas Craig	Rudolph Bunner	John Huling
6th Pa.	Robert Magaw	Josiah Harmar	Jeremiah Talbot
9th Pa.	Richard Butler	Matthew Smith	Francis Nichols
12th Pa.	Wm. Cooke	Neigel Gray	
Continental	Wm. Malcolm	Aaron Burr	Albert Pawling
Continental	Oliver Spencer	Ebenezer Lindsley	

Brig. Gen. Jedediah Huntington's Brigade

5th Conn.	Philip B. Bradley	Matthew Mead	Jonathon Johnson
2d Conn.	Charles Webb	Isaac Sherman	Hezekiah Holdridge
7th Conn.	Heman Swift		John Sedgwick

Brig. Gen. James M. Varnum's Brigade

1st R.I.	Christopher Greene	Adam Comstock	Samuel Ward
2d R.I.	Israel Angell	Jeremiah Olney	Simeon Thayer
8th Conn.	John Chandler	Thomas Dyer	David Smith
4th Conn.	John Durkee	Giles Russell	

Brig. Gen. Lachlan McIntosh's Brigade

1st N.C.	Thomas Clark	Wm. Davis	John Walker and James Emmet
2d N.C.	John Patten	Selby Harney	Hardy Murfree
4th N.C.	Thomas Polk	James Thackston	John Armstrong
3d N.C.	Jethro Sumner	Caleb Brewster	Henry Dixon
5th N.C.	Edward Buncombe	Wm. L. Davidson	Thomas Hogg
6th N.C.	Gideon Lamb	Wm. Taylor	John B. Ashe
8th N.C.	James Armstrong	Levi Dawson	Pinketham Eaton
7th N.C.	James Hogun	Robert Mebane	Wm. Fenner
9th N.C.	John P. Williams	John Luttrell	Wm. Polk

Brig. Gen. Henry Knox's Artillery Brigade*

1st Cont. Art.	Charles Harrison	Edward Carrington	Christian Holmer
2d Cont. Art.	John Lamb	Eleazer Oswald	Sebastian Bauman
3d Cont. Art.	John Crane	John Popkin	
4th Cont. Art.	Thomas Proctor	John Strobagh	Thomas Forrest

The following two regiments appear to have not been attached to any of the Brigades.

Continental	David Henley	Wm. Tudor	Wm. Curtis
Continental	Henry Jackson	David Cobb	John S. Tyler

Note.—Most of the four regiments of the Continental Dragoons, parts of two regiments of Artillery Artificers, and of the Engineers and Sappers and Miners were there, but the specific data is incomplete.

---

*Only parts of the 1st and 2d Continental Artillery were at Valley Forge.

ORDER OF BATTLE, JULY, 1781.

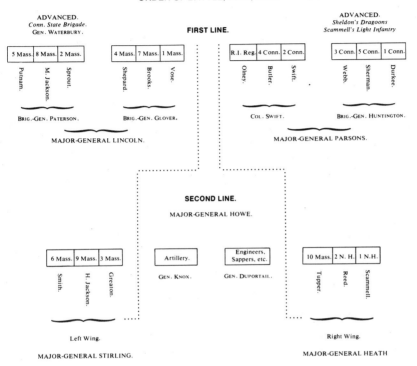

ADVANCED.
Conn. State Brigade.
GEN. WATERBURY.

FIRST LINE.

ADVANCED.
Sheldon's Dragoons
Scammell's Light Infantry

| 5 Mass. | 8 Mass. | 2 Mass. | | 4 Mass. | 7 Mass. | 1 Mass. | | R.I. Reg. | 4 Conn. | 2 Conn. | | 3 Conn. | 5 Conn. | 1 Conn. |

Putnam. | M. Jackson. | Sprout. | Shepard. | Brooks. | Vose. | Olney. | Butler. | Swift. | Webb. | Sherman. | Durkee.

BRIG.-GEN. PATERSON.   BRIG.-GEN. GLOVER.   COL. SWIFT.   BRIG.-GEN. HUNTINGTON.

MAJOR-GENERAL LINCOLN.   MAJOR-GENERAL PARSONS.

SECOND LINE.

MAJOR-GENERAL HOWE.

| 6 Mass. | 9 Mass. | 3 Mass. | | Artillery. | | Engineers, Sappers, etc. | | 10 Mass. | 2 N.H. | 1 N.H. |

Smith. | H. Jackson. | Greaton. | GEN. KNOX. | GEN. DUPORTAIL. | Tupper. | Reed. | Scammell.

Left Wing.   Right Wing.

MAJOR-GENERAL STIRLING.   MAJOR-GENERAL HEATH

General Washington, Commander-in-Chief.

ORDER OF BATTLE, AUG. — OCT., 1782.

| N. H. Brig. | 1st Mass. Brig. Col. Shepherd. | 2d Mass. Brig. Gen. Paterson. | 3d Mass. Brig. Col. Greaton. | | 2d Conn. Brig. Col. Swift. | 1st Conn. Brig. Gen. Huntington. | N. Y. Brig. Col. Cortlandt. | N. J. Brig. Col. Dayton. |

MAJ.-GEN. STIRLING'S DIVISION.   MAJ.-GEN. HOWE'S DIVISION.   MAJ.-GEN. MCDOUGALL'S DIVISION.   MAJ.-GEN. ST. CLAIR DIVISION.

Left Wing.   Right Wing.
MAJ.-GEN. HEATH.   MAJ.-GEN. GATES.

HIS EXCELLENCY, GEN. WASHINGTON, COMMANDER-IN-CHIEF.

FOOTNOTES

1. *Journals of the Continental Congress* (Washington, 1908), XIII, 42.
2. Harold L. Peterson, *The Book of the Continental Soldier* (Harrisburg, 1968), p. 268.
3. *Journals of the Continental Congress,* XI, 642.
4. *Archives of Maryland* (Baltimore, 1900), XVIII, 594.
5. Henry Lee, *Memoirs of the War in the Southern Department of the United States* (New York, 1869), pp. 181-182.
6. George Washington, *The Writings of Washington* (Washington, 1931-1944), XXVII, 229.
7. Peterson, *Book of the Continental Soldier,* p. 270.
8. *Connecticut Military Record 1775-1848* (Hartford, 1889), p. 91.
9. Peterson, *Book of the Continental Soldier,* p. 264.
10. *Journals of the Continental Congress,* VIII, 730.
11. Washington, X, 277.
12. *Journals of the Continental Congress,* X, 148.
13. *Journals of the Continental Congress,* XV, 1398.
14. *Journals of the Continental Congress,* XII, 1103.
15. Francis B. Heitman, *List of Officers of the United States Army* (New York, 1900), no page numbers.
16. *Journals of the Continental Congress, XXII,* 296.
17. *Connecticut Military Record,* p. 124.
18. *Journals of the Continental Congress,* VIII, 730.
19. Heitman.
20. Washington, X, 279.
21. Heitman.
22. Washington, VII, 245.
23. *Journals of the Continental Congress,* IV, 39.
24. *Connecticut Military Record,* p. 110.
25. *Journals of the Continental Congress,* III, 335.

26. *Journals of the Continental Congress,* III, 450.
27. *Journals of the Continental Congress,* IV, 75.
28. *Archives of Maryland,* XVIII, 596.
29. *Connecticut Military Record,* p. 260.
30. Washington, XX, 277-281.
31. Washington, XXIV, 352.
32. Washington, XXV, 466.
33. Washington, XXVI, 497.
34. *Journals of the Continental Congress,* XIII, 58.
35. Ibid.
36. *Journals of the Continental Congress,* V, 476.
37. Peterson, *Book of the Continental Soldier,* p. 254; William A. Ganoe, *The History of the United States Army* (New York, 1942), p. 4.
38. *Connecticut Military Record,* p. 301.
39. *Connecticut Military Record,* p. 311.
40. Peterson, *Book of the Continental Soldier,* p. 254.
41. Harold L. Peterson, *Round Shot and Rammers* (Harrisburg, 1969), p. 66.
42. Peterson, *Round Shot and Rammers,* p. 57.
43. *Journals of the Continental Congress,* IV, 212.
44. *Journals of the Continental Congress,* IV, 365.
45. Peterson, *Book of the Continental Soldier,* p. 261.
46. Washington, X, 279.
47. Washington, XXIV, 352.
48. Peterson, *Book of the Continental Soldier,* p. 262.
49. *Connecticut Military Record,* p. 284.
50. Washington, X, 279.
51. Washington, X, 279.
52. Peterson, *Book of the Continental Soldier,* p. 262.
53. Peterson, *Book of the Continental Soldier,* p. 197.
54. *Colonial Records of Pennsylvania* (Harrisburg, 1852), X, 685.
55. Peterson, *Book of the Continental Soldier,* p. 262.
56. Washington, X, 279.
57. Peterson, *Book of the Continental Soldier,* p. 267.
58. *Journals of the Continental Congress,* XIV, 659
59. *Journals of the Continental Congress,* XVI, 156.
60. Washington, XX, 277-281.
61. Peterson, *Book of the Continental Soldier,* p. 266.
62. Washington, X, 362-399.
63. Peterson, *Book of the Continental Soldier,* p. 268.
64. *Journals of the Continental Congress,* VI, 1025.
65. Washington, X, 362-399.
66. Washington, XXVI, 497.
67. Washington, X, 362-399.
68. Lee, p. 208.
69. Lee, pp. 171, 208.
70. Lee, p. 552.
71. Washington, XXV, 466.
72. *Connecticut Military Record,* p. 106.
73. *Delaware Archives, Military* (Wilmington, 1911), I, 31.
74. Lee, p. 185.
75. J. Thomas Scharf, *History of Maryland* (Hatboro, 1967), II, 384.

Footnotes

76. Lee, p. 552
77. *Archives of Maryland,* XVIII, 365.
78. *Journals of the Continental Congress,* XIII, 58.
79. *Journals of the Continental Congress,* IV, 239.
80. *Connecticut Military Record,* p. 263.
81. *Connecticut Military Record,* p. 113.
82. *Journals of the Continental Congress,* IV, 239.
83. Washington, X, 279.

84. Washington, XII, 30-32.
85. Washington, XXVI, 443; *Journals of the Continental Congress,* XXV, 625.
86. Washington, XVI, 65.
87. *Archives of Maryland,* XVIII, 429.
88. *Official Letters of the Governors of Virginia* (Richmond, 1926), I, 221.
89. *Journals of the Continental Congress,* II, 93.
90. *Journals of the Continental Congress,* V, 606.
91. *Journals of the Continental Congress,* X, 160.
92. Kenneth Coleman, *The American Revolution in Georgia* (Athens, 1958), p. 103.
93. *Journals of the Continental Congress,* XVI, 156.
94. Lucian Lamar Knight, *Georgia's Roster of the Revolution* (Baltimore, 1967), pp. 13-14.
95. *Revolutionary Records of Georgia* (Atlanta, 1908), III, 161.
96. Washington, XXV, 162.
97. *Revolutionary Records of Georgia,* III, 262.
98. *Journals of the Continental Congress,* V, 521.
99. *Journals of the Continental Congress,* X, 160.
100. *Revolutionary Records of Georgia,* II, 185.
101. *Revolutionary Records of Georgia,* II, 326.

102. *Journals of the Continental Congress,* V, 486.
103. *Journals of the Continental Congress,* V, 571.
104. Washington, XI, 347.
105. *Archives of Maryland,* XVIII, 594.
106. Lee, p. 552.

107. *Archives of Maryland,* XVIII, 596.
108. *Archives of Maryland,* XVIII, 596.
109. *Journals of the Continental Congress,* XIII, 58.
110. *Journals of the Continental Congress,* IV, 241.
111. *Documentary History of the American Revolution* (New York, 1857), II, 108.
112. *Documentary History of the American Revolution,* II, 135.
113. *Documentary History of South Carolina* (Columbia, 1853), p. 168.
114. *Documentary History of South Carolina,* p. 186.
115. *Documentary History of South Carolina,* p. 270.
116. *Documentary History of South Carolina,* p. 279.
117. *Journals of the Continental Congress,* VIII, 380.
118. *Journals of the Continental Congress,* IV, 241.
119. *Journals of the Continental Congress,* XVI, 118.
120. *Journals of the Continental Congress,* VIII, 380.
121. *Journals of the Continental Congress,* VIII, 485, 555.
122. *Journals of the Continental Congress,* XXIV, 321.
123. Washington, XIX, 206.

124. Washington, XVII, 124.
125. Edward McCrady, *The History of South Carolina in the Revolution* (New York, 1901-1902), I, 509.
126. *Connecticut Military Record*, pp. 121-122.
127. Peterson, *Book of the Continental Soldier*, pp. 261-262.
128. *Journals of the Continental Congress*, VII, 46.
129. Peterson, *Book of the Continental Soldier*, p. 254.
130. *Journals of the Continental Congress*, V, 521.
131. *Revolutionary Records of Georgia*, II, 38.
132. Peterson, *Book of the Continental Soldier*, p. 270.
133. Lee, p. 552.
134. Washington, X, 279.
135. *Journals of the Continental Congress*, XIX, 148.
136. *Archives of Maryland*, XVIII, 4.
137. Scharf, p. 356.
138. Scharf, p. 384.
139. *Archives of Maryland*, XVIII, 429.
140. *Archives of Maryland*, XVIII, 4.
141. Scharf, p. 384.
142. Washington, XIX, 85, 207.
143. Scharf, p. 384.
144. Scharf, p. 384.
145. Peterson, *Book of the Continental Soldier*, p. 254.
146. Washington, V, 96.
147. Washington, XXV, 461.
148. *Documentary History of South Carolina*, p. 238.
149. *Documentary History of South Carolina*, pp. 270, 281.
150. *Journals of the Continental Congress*, XIII, 58.
151. Washington, XV, 345; Peterson, *Book of the Continental Soldier*, p. 270.
152. *Journals of the Continental Congress*, IV, 174.
153. *Journals of the Continental Congress*, V, 521.
154. *Journals of the Continental Congress*, IV, 101.
155. Washington, XII, 341.
156. *New Hampshire State Papers* (Concord, 1874), VIII, 45.
157. Ibid.
158. *Journals of the Continental Congress*, V, 618.
159. *Journals of the Continental Congress*, XXV, 802.
160. Washington, XXI, 43, 335.
161. *New Hampshire State Papers*, VII.
162. *Officers and Men of New Jersey in the Revolutionary War* (Trenton, 1872), p. 319.
163. Washington, XI, 347.
164. *Journals of the Continental Congress*, III, 335.
165. *Journals of the Continental Congress*, IV, 123.
166. *Journals of the Continental Congress*, XIX, 339.
167. Washington, X, 399.
168. Peterson, *Book of the Continental Soldier*, p. 254.
169. *Journals of the Continental Congress*, IV, 190.
170. *Journals of the Continental Congress*, V, 480.
171. *Records of the Revolutionary War* (New York, 1858), p. 161.
172. *Journals of the Continental Congress*, IV, 39.

Footnotes

173. *Journals of the Continental Congress*, IV, 332.
174. Washington, IX, 117.
175. Washington, IX, 117-119.
176. *Journals of the Continental Congress*, VIII, 730.
177. *The Bland Papers*, p. 97.
178. *Colonial Records of North Carolina* (Raleigh, 1890), X, 187.
179. *Colonial Records of North Carolina*, X, 514.
180. *State Records of North Carolina* (Winston, 1896), XIII, 531; *Journals of the Continental Congress*, XI, 550.
181. R.D.W. Connor, *History of North Carolina* (New York, 1919), I, 485.
182. *State Records of North Carolina*, XVI, 725.
183. *Journals of the Continental Congress*, VI, 1007.
184. *Journals of the Continental Congress*, IV, 29.
185. *Journals of the Continental Congress*, II, 104.
186. Washington, XXII, 258.
187. *Journals of the Continental Congress*, XXII, 148.
188. *Journals of the Continental Congress*, VII, 21.
189. *Journals of the Continental Congress*, X, 312.
190. Peterson, *Book of the Continental Soldier*, p. 270.
191. *Journals of the Continental Congress*, XIX, 182.
192. Ibid; Washington, XVII, 496.
193. *Official Letters of the Governors of Virginia*, I, 96.
194. Washington, XIV, 180.
195. Washington, XIV, 347.
196. Scharf, p. 356.
197. *Rhode Island Colonial Records* (Providence, 1863), VII, 314.
198. *Rhode Island Colonial Records*, VII, 322.
199. *Journals of the Continental Congress*, VII, 46.
200. *Journals of the Continental Congress*, II, 93-94.
201. Washington, V, 286.
202. *Journals of the Continental Congress*, V, 571.
203. *Journals of the Continental Congress*, VII, 21.
204. *Extracts from the Journals of the Provincial Congresses 1775-1776* (Columbia, 1960), p. 203.
205. *Extracts*, p. 40.
206. *Journals of the Continental Congress*, III, 325.
207. *Documentary History of South Carolina*, p. 6.
208. *Documentary History of the American Revolution*, II, 97.
209. *Documentary History of the American Revolution*, II, 133.
210. *Extracts*, p. 43.
211. *Journals of the Continental Congress*, V, 606.
212. *Extracts*, p. 124.
213. *Extracts*, p. 203.
214. *Extracts*, p. 212.
215. *Journals of the Continental Congress*, IV, 174.
216. *Connecticut Military Record*, p. 263.
217. *Journals of the Continental Congress*, II, 220.
218. *Journals of the Continental Congress*, XIV, 601.
219. *Journals of the Continental Congress*, IV, 364-365.
220. *Journals of the Continental Congress*, VIII, 245.
221. *Journals of the Continental Congress*, XVIII, 878.

222. *Journals of the Continental Congress*, II, 220.
223. *Journals of the Continental Congress*, XXI, 1093.
224. *Journals of the Continental Congress*, XXII, 410.
225. *Journals of the Continental Congress*, IV, 235.
226. *Journals of the Continental Congress*, II, 93-94.
227. *Journals of the Continental Congress*, IV, 151.
228. *Journals of the Continental Congress*, VI, 1050.
229. *Connecticut Military Record*, p. 289.
230. Washington, XVIII, 1.
231. *Journals of the Continental Congress*, XXII, 235.
232. *Journals of the Continental Congress*, XVI, 301.
233. *Journals of the Continental Congress*, V, 486.
234. *Journals of the Continental Congress*, X, 150.
235. Washington, V, 185.
236. *The Virginia Magazine of History and Biography*, XX, No. 1 (1912), 65.
237. Peterson, *Book of the Continental Soldier*, p. 197.
238. *Virginia Magazine of History and Biography*, XX, No. 1, 67.
239. *Virginia Magazine of History and Biography*, XX, No. 2, 184.
240. *Virginia Magazine of History and Biography*, XX, No. 3, 268.
241. *Official Letters of the Governors of Virginia*, I, 96.
242. *Journals of the Continental Congress*, XV, 1366.
243. Washington, XXII, 343.
244. Washington, XXIV, 164-165.
245. Washington, XXVII, 177.
246. *Connecticut Military Record*, p. 109.
247. *Journals of the Continental Congress*, V, 518.
248. Carlos E. Godfrey, *The Commander in Chief's Life Guard* (Washington, 1904), passim.
249. *Journals of the Continental Congress*, IV, 212.
250. *Revolutionary Records of Georgia*, II, 38.

Bibliography

ARCHIVAL MATERIALS:
General:
Bland Papers.
Journals of the Continental Congress. Washington: Government Printing Office, 1908.
Records of the Revolutionary War. New York: Pudney and Russell, 1858.
Washington, George. *The Writings of Washington.* Washington: 1944.

Connecticut:
Connecticut Military Record 1775-1848. Hartford, 1889.

Delaware:
Delaware Archives, Military. Wilmington: Press of Mercantile Printing Company, 1911.

Georgia:
Knight, Lucian Lamar. *Georgia's Roster of the Revolution.* Baltimore: Genealogical Publishing Company, 1967.
Revolutionary Records of Georgia. Atlanta: Chandler, 1908.

Maryland:
Archives of Maryland. Baltimore: Maryland Historical Society, 1900.

New Hampshire:
New Hampshire State Papers. Concord: Charles C. Person, 1874.

New Jersey:
Officers and Men of New Jersey in the Revolutionary War. Trenton: William T. Nicholson and Company, 1872.

North Carolina:
Colonial Records of North Carolina. Raleigh: Josephus Daniels, 1890.
State Records of North Carolina. Winston: Walter Clark, 1896.

Pennsylvania:
Colonial Records of Pennsylvania. Harrisburg: Theodore Fenn and Company, 1852.
Pennsylvania Archives. Philadelphia: J.S. Severns, 1853.

Rhode Island:
Rhode Island Colonial Records. Providence: Cooke, Jackson, and Company, 1863.

South Carolina:
Extracts from the Journals of the Provincial Congresses 1775-1776. Columbia: South Carolina Archives Department, 1960.
Documentary History of the American Revolution. New York: Appleton and Company, 1854.

Documentary History of South Carolina. Columbia: Banner Steam-Power Press, 1853.

Virginia:
Official Letters of the Governors of Virginia. Richmond: Virginia State Library, 1926.
Statutes at Large of All the Laws of Virginia. Richmond: George Cochran, 1822.

OTHER PRIMARY SOURCES
Grose, Francis. *Military Antiquities.* London: , 1801.
Lee, Henry. *Memoirs of the War in the Southern Department of the United States.* New York: University Publishing Company, 1869.
Pennsylvania Gazette 1775-May, 1781.
Virginia Gazette 1775-1780.
Von Steuben, Friedrich Wilhelm. *Regulations for the Order and Discipline of the Troops of the United States.* Edition unknown, but may be 1779.

SECONDARY SOURCES
Boatner, Mark Mayo, III. *Encyclopedia of the American Revolution.* New York: David McKay Company, 1966.
Coleman, Kenneth. *The American Revolution in Georgia.* Athens: University of Georgia Press, 1958.
Conner, R.D.W. *History of North Carolina.* New York: Lewis Publishing Company, 1919.
Fortescue, John. *History of the British Army.* London: Macmillan, 1910.
Ganoe, William Addleman. *The History of the United States Army.* New York: D. Appleton-Century Company, 1942.
Godfrey, Carlos E. *The Commander in Chief's Life Guard.* Washington: Stevenson-Smith Company, 1904.
Heitman, Francis B. *Historical Register of Officers of the Continental Army*, Washington: Rare Book Shop Publishing Company, 1914.
Heitman, Francis B. *List of Officers of the United States Army 1776-1900.* New York: L.R. Hamersly, 1900.
Johnston, Henry P. *The Yorktown Campaign and the Surrender of Cornwallis.* New York: Harper and Brothers, 1881.
Journal of the Company of Military Historians
McCrady, Edward. *The History of South Carolina in the Revolution.* New York: Macmillan Company, 1902.
Moore, George H. *Employment of Negroes in the American Army of the Revolution.* New York: Charles T. Evans, 1862.
Peterson, Harold L. *The Book of the Continental Soldier.* Harrisburg: Stackpole Books, 1968.
Peterson, Harold L. *Round Shot and Rammers.* Harrisburg: Stackpole Books, 1969.
Quarles, Benjamin. *The Negro in the American Revolution.* Chapel Hill: University of North Carolina Press, 1961.
Rankin, Hugh F. *The North Carolina Continentals.* Chapel Hill: University of North Carolina Press, 1971.
Scharf, J. Thomas. *History of Maryland.* Hatboro: Tradition Press, 1967.
Tyler, Lyon Gardiner. *History of Virginia.* New York: American Historical Society, 1924.
Virginia Magazine of History and Biography.

Index of Names

Index